The Woman's
Book of Orgasm

The Woman's Book of Orgasm

A Guide to the Ultimate Sexual Pleasure

Edited by Tara Barker

Citadel Press
Kensington Publishing Corp.
www.kensingtonbooks.com

CITADEL PRESS books are published by

Kensington Publishing Corp.
850 Third Avenue
New York, NY 10022

Originally published in Great Britain in 1997 by Michael O'Mara Books
Limited, under the title *The Book of the Orgasm.*

All Kensington titles, imprints, and distributed lines are available at special
quantity discounts for bulk purchases for sales promotions, premiums,
fund raising, educational, or institutional use. Special book excerpts or
customized printings can also be created to fit specific needs. For details,
write or phone the office of the Kensington special sales manager:
Kensington Publishing Corp., 850 Third Avenue, New York, NY 10022,
attn: Special Sales Department, phone 1-800-221-2647.

Kensington and the K logo Reg. U.S. Pat. & TM Office
Citadel Press is a trademark of Kensington Publishing Corp.

First printing 1997

10 9 8

Printed in the United States of America

Library of Congress Cataloging-in-Publication Data

The woman's book of orgasm : a guide to the ultimate sexual pleasure/
edited by Tara Barker.
     p.   cm.
   ISBN 0–8065–1966–5
    1. Sex instruction for women.   2. Women—Sexual behavior.
  3. Female orgasm.   I. Barker, Tara.
  HQ46.W66   1998
  613.9'6—dc21   97–32606
                                                CIP

CONTENTS

Preface

Are you ready for the ultimate pleasure? Real women share the secrets of their orgasm

Relationship experts know the link between sexual enjoyment and a happy, confident life. That's why it's as important to enjoy pleasure in bed as it is to expect a fulfilling career and an enjoyable social life. All too often, however, self-consciousness or stress can get in the way of excitement. That's why this book is dedicated to your ultimate sexual pleasure – a really thrilling orgasm.

And while we're on the subject, it's worth noting that this book is unique – because it's filled with the experiences of real-life young women, not just tips from sex experts.

In every chapter real women like you talk about their own sex lives. They share the positions they like (and don't), detail their favourite masturbation techniques, foreplay successes, favourite sexual fantasies – you name it – and above all they give new insight into how every woman can have more frequent and more thrilling orgasms.

In case you're wondering how such candid information was gathered, we asked the readers of *Company* magazine, the leading British glossy magazine for women in their twenties. Replying to questions in the magazine, hundreds of readers wrote in, sharing their thoughts and desires, and what came through clear and strong is that young women today are different.

Unlike women of previous generations we feel we have a right to an enjoyable, intimate, loving sex life – and we're willing to do our part to make sure we get one.

So, in the quest for more enjoyable sex, plus more delicious orgasms, settle back, relax and remember the first rule of pleasure: be you, be free, be safe, but most of all, ENJOY!

Chapter 1

A REAL NEED (OH BABY . . .)

→ The physical and evolutionary reasons behind your orgasm

→ Multiple to mental – there's not just one kind of orgasm

→ Anatomy of an orgasm – the machinery behind those exquisite shudders

'My orgasm starts off as a small pulsating feeling in my vagina which becomes more intense. At the peak the contractions are really fast and the pulsating feeling fans out through my whole body and I feel hot and flushed. I don't have a single thought in my head, everything concentrates on that intensity.'

Grace

'If I have an orgasm through intercourse I feel emotionally connected with my partner and would like to continue kissing and cuddling afterwards. If I have an orgasm through my partner's oral or manual stimulation everything feels more intense and urgent. I feel almost euphoric when I orgasm this way.'

Rachel

●→ Do orgasms have a purpose?

Orgasms are bliss, but biologically speaking, there's no real reason why women have them. In nature, sex exists for one reason: survival of the species. Sexual pleasure is a side effect. It may seem unfair, but the male orgasm makes biological sense. In nearly every case his orgasm is triggered by intercourse, leads to ejaculation, and this, in turn, can lead to fertilisation of the egg and eventually, a baby.

During orgasm the contraction of muscles lining the reproductive tract propels sperm up from the testes and out through the penis, and once the penis is inside the vagina the forceful action of orgasm helps push the sperm up towards the cervix, the entrance to the uterus or womb. So, in a very real way, the pleasure of the male orgasm helps ensure the continuation of the species.

Female sexuality is more complex. For a start, we don't need an orgasm to get pregnant. Even more baffling, the clitoris – the trigger to women's orgasm – is not very well placed when it comes to penis-in-vagina or 'penetrative' sex.

A design flaw?

If sex was really unpleasant for women, we'd probably never bother to do it, and that way we'd never get pregnant. Relationship expert Dr Andrew Stanway explains: 'Female sexual response is designed to make sex attractive enough to overcome the downside – the pain of giving birth and the commitment of nurturing children for a long time.'

So do our orgasms exist to encourage us to have sex and make babies?

Well, not quite – because our orgasms aren't very closely linked to intercourse. After all, if the female orgasm was designed to make us crave intercourse, surely the clitoris would be inside the vagina? Perhaps there are good biological reasons why men and women don't easily have simultaneous orgasms: some experts believe that if Stone Age men and women were completely sexually abandoned at the same time, neither would have been on the lookout for sabre-tooth tigers.

Other experts believe humans, unlike other animals, are designed for face-to-face sex. First, because eye contact is an important sexual signal to us. Second, face-to-face contact ensures some chance of friction on the clitoris during sex. It may also help bond the man and woman so they are willing to invest years of time and effort on their children.

So could there be a physical link between female orgasm and reproduction after all? Possibly. During the muscular contractions of the female orgasm, the cervix actually dips down in the seminal fluid with a sipping motion. The womb's rippling contractions may also help suck up sperm, and propel them up towards the Fallopian tubes, where fertilisation actually takes place. Experts aren't sure yet if this helps conception, but it may do.

Scientists studying female orgasms have also seen the vagina 'tent' during orgasm – in other words, the vaginal walls, which are normally floppy like a collapsed balloon, suddenly arch up like a pitched tent. The result is that the cervix is revealed like a giant bull's eye. This may help us get pregnant as it would make it easier for sperm to enter the womb, but again, experts aren't sure.

If we don't need orgasms to reproduce, and our sexual thrills don't come primarily from penetrative sex, what's going on? It may be that nature threw the female orgasm in as a sweetener to keep women interested in having sex. It may also be true that orgasms play an important role in keeping men and women together long-term, and having two loving parents makes it easier to raise children. After all, the extreme pleasure in giving and getting an orgasm is a strong bond between a couple, and a woman who finds a man who can help her have mind-blowing orgasms is unlikely to give him up easily.

➻ The anatomy of an orgasm

There is an incredible machinery behind the exquisite shudders of your orgasm, and the changes to your body during arousal and orgasm are truly fascinating. Although the orgasm itself can feel like an explosion, it's actually the climax of several stages.

Stage 1: Arousal

Within 10 to 30 seconds of becoming aroused, glands at the opening of your vagina – called Bartholin's glands – begin secreting a mucus-like lubricating fluid and blood rushes to the pelvic area. Your rising body temperature may lead to what's called an 'orgasm flush' or a reddening of your neck and chest. The labia minora (the inner lips of the vagina) also become engorged with blood in the same way that blood rushing to the penis can cause an erection. At the same time, glands in the walls of the vagina secrete a clear fluid that lubricates the inner tissues. Some women produce a lot, while others need the help of vaginal lubricants to ensure comfortable penetration. This is partly due to how aroused a woman becomes; feelings like tiredness or anxiety inhibit arousal. If dryness is a problem for you, keep a water-based lubricant on hand (available without prescription from the chemist).

The blood rushing to the vulva (the entire outside area of the vagina) darkens its appearance. In white women it can change from pink to dark red, in darker women it can become almost purple. As foreplay continues, your clitoris (a hard bump at the top of the entrance of the vagina, nestling in the folds of skin where the labia minora meet) swells and hardens. Meanwhile the inner part of your vagina (which is normally much like a long, collapsed balloon) lengthens and barrels out around the cervix, the ring of muscle which forms the gateway to the uterus or womb. The uterus tilts backwards, causing the upper part of the vagina to stretch in preparation for accommodating a penis. The arousal phase usually takes about 15 minutes, although frequently it can take up to 25 minutes – biological proof that wham-bam sex does not satisfy most women.

Stage 2: Plateau

As sexual tension increases you'll enter the plateau

stage, where you long to feel satisfied. If penetration occurs before this stage, your partner's initial thrusts may feel painful. However, the vagina continues to expand rapidly regardless of the size of your lover's penis, so it's usually soon comfortably accommodated. Very occasionally, with increasing excitement, the vagina can over-extend itself in width and length so it loses its firm grip on the penis, leading some women to feel less sensation as the penis feels 'lost' inside them. However, most of the vagina's nerve endings are in the outer third (nearest the opening), proving penis length isn't that important. As it thrusts in and out, the movement of the body back and forth releases the clitoral hood, a small protective hood of skin that is usually tucked away behind the sensitive clitoris. The clitoris itself is the key to a woman's orgasm – it used to be thought it was just a pea-sized bump of tissue, but now scientists know this tiny bud is actually like the tip of an iceberg – the top of a collection of nerve endings, many of which fan out around the vulva and down your inner thighs. Like a penis, a clitoris can become erect (see Chapter 2 for more details). During sex, the clitoris stiffens, swells and doubles in size. Sometimes it becomes so stimulated it seems to disappear under the clitoral hood. This is when direct pressure may feel almost painful, but stroking the sides or around it will give you the pleasure you need.

Stage 3: Orgasm

It's still not known what exactly triggers orgasm, although it's clearly the peak of an as yet unmeasured amount of stimulation. We do know that part of the trigger comes from a reflex that's relayed through the brain, so it can be psychologically blocked if you're nervous or inhibited. This is why the more comfortable you are with your partner, and the more you have sex together, the more likely you are to achieve orgasm.

During your orgasm the uterus rises and the upper part of the vagina balloons out. The muscles of the vagina contract every 0.8 seconds, the same frequency as the ejaculations of a man's orgasm. After the first three to six contractions the interval between contractions lengthens and the sensations fade away. For many women the tissues remain engorged, so if you continue to be stimulated you may be able to have multiple orgasms.

Stage 4: Resolution

Once the final contractions fade, the extra blood starts draining away from the pelvic area and the swelling of the engorged tissues goes down. The lubricating fluid is no longer produced and your blood pressure, heart rate and breathing all return to normal. However, your face, neck and shoulders remain flushed because the higher blood pressure during arousal and plateau forces your whole body to work harder. This post-orgasmic glow can be very visible, but it's not different from any other kind of flush, so you won't be giving any secrets away.

This final phase generally takes about 10 to 15 minutes. The drop in blood pressure causes a feeling of deep relaxation and sleep is a natural reaction. Remember, every orgasm is different. There are no rights and wrongs. The fun lies in discovering what your individual reaction is all about.

⇔ Twin peaks

Does his orgasm feel different from hers, or are we all the same when pleasure peaks?

A woman describes her orgasm

'When I first meet someone I want to have sex with I feel a throbbing ache low down in my stomach. The feeling builds until we get into foreplay. Once I get this I know I'm getting wet. If the man is someone new I want to sleep with, just kissing him is enough to get me ready. If he's a regular partner it takes a bit longer to get warmed up. Foreplay is great, but a man should move on if something gets boring. Men say they can't tell when that is, but it's easy: you start to get dry. Female orgasms require concentration, you have to be mentally turned on and relaxed.

'I'd say I have three kinds of orgasm: vaginal, clitoral and multiple. When I orgasm vaginally through sex, the climaxes are less intense. Initially, I'll feel empty, like I want to be filled up – which is why the moment of penetration is often the best as it satisfies that need immediately. The feeling of sexual need then grows stronger and stronger until I climax.

'Clitoral orgasms are much sharper – the excitement and tension are more focused on the vaginal area. One second before I come I feel a rush of heat, then my vagina goes into spasms. While I'm having the contractions it's better if he stops stimulating me directly and just maintains the pressure. I'm so sensitive at that point that it can hurt if he's too enthusiastic.

'Although one orgasm is enough, I can have more if we continue to make love. When it comes to multiple orgasms, the second or third is often the best. If I'm in the mood, it doesn't take me long to climax, and the whole thing lasts about six to ten seconds with five or six major contractions and lots of little ones afterwards. The most frustrating thing about orgasms is that sometimes I'm on the brink and then get distracted, which can easily happen. If my partner does something wrong, or changes what he's doing, it can put me off and I know I'll never have one. Whatever he's doing, it has to be gentle, insistent pressure.

'Afterwards I feel physically sensitive and ticklish and sometimes quite embarrassed, if I'm with someone new. It takes me a few minutes to come back to earth – if I get up immediately I feel faint so I lie there for a bit.'

A man describes his orgasm

'For me, orgasm starts well before a woman touches me. If I know I'm going to have sex that night I'm excited all day. Even if I'm not thinking about it consciously I'll get an erection. I love the build-up: the talking, flirting and foreplay. I love the feeling of being erect. Usually arousal happens before you know it: in seconds I'm primed. I can feel my testicles lifting up and there's a hot feeling below chest level. This excited state is the best and I try to prolong it.

'If it's the first time, I worry whether I'm going to live up to expectations. Generally though, the longer the build-up, the better. A rushed orgasm can feel a bit empty. At the moment before orgasm I can definitely feel a build-up of fluid. At that point, even if I stop moving, I can ejaculate without having an orgasm. The semen comes out, but I don't have any of the pleasure associated with it. To get the most out of an orgasm, you have to link the physical actions of your body with what's going on in your head.

'Orgasm is a definite release of energy: like desperately needing to go to the toilet, and then letting go. The orgasm itself feels like waves of pleasure. It's not one continual thing – you can feel yourself pumping. It's intense – it only lasts for six seconds or less – but even at the most crucial point I'm conscious of whether my partner's enjoying it or not.

'My best orgasms happen when I'm having sex a lot. If you haven't had sex for ages, the reality never lives up to your expectations, and you're not so able to control your orgasm. That's why sometimes, if I haven't had sex in ages and know 'I'm going to that night, I masturbate during the day to take the edge off it. Then the orgasm at night seems to last longer and you produce more fluid. On the other hand, I once spent all day in bed and had sex five times. At the end I felt like nothing was coming out. I was still having orgasms though and they felt great – although the first is always the best. I don't notice a huge difference between most orgasms, but the ones from oral sex feel different: much more intense but less violent.

'If I had to describe my orgasm in three words, I'd say they're powerful, intense and wet. After I've climaxed, I feel satisfied and have to rest for at least half an hour. Once I've come, my penis is back to normal within a few minutes. Emotionally, there's nothing better than having an orgasm with someone you love. Orgasm can be a physical and emotional thing – the physical side is pretty much always the same, the emotional is different depending on who you're with.'

Chapter 2

WELCOME TO THE PLEASURE ZONES

➡ Your erogenous zones – from your clitoris to the recently discovered A Spot

➡ Female erections – and how they can bring new excitement to your love-making

➡ Hormones and your sex drive

'Oral sex is my favourite way to climax. It's very intense and the contractions feel hard and fierce. I also sometimes experience orgasms through penetrative sex. They're not so powerful, perhaps because his penis is in the way of the contractions. But I still enjoy them.'

Katharine

'My orgasm is definitely affected by my mood. If I'm feeling really horny I come quickly and powerfully. If I'm tense or angry it's just like a little sneeze. More of a release of tension than a wave of pleasure. I do feel more relaxed afterwards though.'

Amanda

➻ Discover your erogenous zones

There's a bedroom full of different ways to experience pleasure. Some orgasms make you shudder, others make you giggle.

We tend to think there is just one kind of orgasm – perhaps it's all the sex scenes we see in movies, where the leading lady screams with delight at the point of orgasm. Real life is far more varied. The sensation of orgasm can be anything from a fleeting flutter to a massive explosion. You might orgasm once or peak several times. You might scream and jerk, or stay silent and still. And you might have three major muscle contractions or fifteen tiny ones. It's all extremely individual.

Your orgasms can also vary from day to day, depending on how comfortable you feel in the relationship, or how tired, excited or relaxed you feel. For example, on Monday you might have a quiet, fluttering orgasm, yet on Tuesday you might have to be peeled off the ceiling after a force ten climax. The female orgasm is what you might call holistic, in that it reflects everything that's going on in your life and your body on that particular day.

From breasts to feet – your individual triggers

Just as the feeling itself varies from woman to woman, so do the triggers. Some women can orgasm just by having their feet massaged. Some women say having their breasts touched makes them climax – others find it boring. Some sex therapists even say women are the superior sex when it comes to orgasm, in that just about anywhere on our body can give us sexual pleasure – and several can help us orgasm.

For a lot of women, the psychological aspects of sex are also important when it comes to having an orgasm. For example, your hair might not be a traditional erogenous zone, but if having your hair stroked feels like affection and love to you, that might make you feel more relaxed – which, in turn, might make it easier for you to have an orgasm.

How long does an orgasm last?

In the movies the leading actress is writhing away for minutes at a time, but in real life orgasms are so intense we feel they last a lot longer than they actually do. In women, one study showed that although their orgasms lasted between 13 and 51 seconds, some women believed their orgasms had lasted between 7 and 107 seconds. For men, the average length of an orgasm is 10 to 30 seconds. Why some orgasms last longer than others has yet to be established.

The hot G Spot

Many of us are still hunting for our G Spot (named after Dr Grafenberg, the German doctor who discovered it), but for some women it's vital for good sex. Although some sex therapists are sceptical, many believe every woman has a G Spot – a cushion of tissue about two inches up on the front wall of the vagina, behind the pubic bone, where the vagina wraps around the urethra (the tube used to evacuate urine from the bladder).

The theory is that some women have erotically sensitive urethras, which means stroking the area of the vagina that the urethra runs behind will be pleasurable. However, the G Spot is not the quick-fire ecstasy button it's often cracked up to be. For some women, having their G Spot stroked will make it swell and pulse with pleasure; other women will feel indifferent, or even irritated.

Bottoms up

As mentioned before, orgasm is a very individual thing – and what excites one woman may leave another cold. For instance, many women would rather run a marathon in high heels than have anal sex, but for others it can lead to orgasm.

International surveys have found that between 12 and 70 per cent of women acknowledge trying anal sex at least once, but the figures between different studies vary wildly as this is an area where it is hard to get people to be entirely honest.

However, what's true is that the anus is loaded with blood vessels and nerve endings, and direct stimulation can trigger climax. Stroking the perineum (the strip of skin between the vaginal opening and the anus) is also stimulating for some women. Emotions come into it as well; as anal sex is still something of a taboo, the feeling that you are doing something 'naughty' and 'forbidden' can be a vital part of the turn-on. (See Chapter 8 for more on this subject.)

Pleasure-zone central – the clitoris

For most women the clitoris is the key to orgasm – virtually all of us can come through stimulation of the clitoris alone.

Psychoanalyst Sigmund Freud came up with the theory that a woman could have two different types of orgasm: clitoral (an orgasm produced by rubbing or touching the clitoris) and vaginal (one produced by the friction of the penis in the vagina, with no direct touching of the clitoris). Freud decided that a clitoral orgasm was inferior in some way. Sex researchers (and most women) now dismiss this theory, pointing out that there's no scientific evidence that some orgasms are 'inferior', and that at least two-thirds of women need direct clitoral stimulation to climax because the inner walls of the vagina have few nerve endings and transmit little sensation. (If the walls were too sensitive, it would be impossible to give birth.)

For about a third of women, the movement of the penis in the vagina creates enough sensation to produce an orgasm, but even this 'vaginal orgasm' involves the clitoris to some extent. During intercourse the vaginal lips are stretched, and because they're attached to the clitoris via connective tissue, the clitoris is stimulated as well. It's this that produces the orgasm.

For most of us the clitoris needs more contact with something – like a finger or tongue – to achieve orgasm. As for one type of orgasm being superior – it's a myth. Neither is better or worse: they're just different paths to pleasure.

M-m-m-multiple orgasms

It's the swings and roundabouts of sex: men can climax faster and pretty much every time, but women can have multiple orgasms. Here's how it works: a multiple orgasm is when you climax but continue to ride a wave of excitement. If you're stimulated during this 'plateau' period you can climax again – and the process can continue for as long as you're willing. It's estimated about a third of women are easily multi-orgasmic. One woman tested had 50 climaxes in a row and only stopped when the testers ran out of male volunteers! However, sex researchers say that nearly all women can become multi-orgasmic, if they practise (and what enjoyable practise . . .).

The reason for this pleasure roller-coaster is that men and women climb towards orgasm in very different ways. For a man, orgasm is like a quick sprint – he peaks quickly and it's all over. Within minutes, sleep hormones kick into his bloodstream and he must rest to build enough energy for the next orgasm. This resting or 'resolution' phase depends on his age (older men need more time to recover) and his level of excitement (a young teenager may need only a few minutes), but on average a man needs about 15 to 30 minutes to get ready for his next orgasm. If you stimulate him during this time he won't get another orgasm and may even find the attention painful.

However, a woman's race to climax is more like a marathon – she climbs towards orgasm more slowly, but once she's up and running she can stay cruising for hours. What's more, sleep hormones and the 'resolution' phase don't kick in for about half an hour after her first climax. Which means if she's stimulated during this time she can have more and more orgasms.

The new A Spot

If you've never heard of this you're not alone; the Anterior Formex Erogenous Zone has only recently been discovered by sex researchers. Located in the front wall of the vagina about a third of the way down from the cervix, it first caused a stir when tests showed that 95 per cent of women who stimulated this spot felt 'erotic sensitivity' and greatly increased vaginal lubrication.

Researchers theorise that rubbing the A Spot causes more blood to flow to the pelvic area, which causes women to lubricate more, and to feel more sexual pleasure. This increased wetness can help some women feel more turned on and more relaxed; both of these can help make it easier to have an orgasm.

Controversy still rages about whether the A Spot exists, or can give women orgasms, but if you're in the mood to try for yourself, here's how to find yours. Wet your fingers and gently slide them up your vagina until you hit the cervix at the back of the vagina. It feels like a firm, yet flexible lump. A few centimetres down you'll find an area that's extremely smooth and sensitive to the touch. That's your A Spot. To stimulate it, slide a finger up and down. To hit the A Spot during intercourse, use a position where the penis contacts the front wall of the vagina, such as the 'doggie' style, or try sitting on the end of the bed while your lover stands between your legs.

Mind games

Some women can climax with no physical stimulation at all. Many of us have 'wet dreams', known medically as 'nocturnal orgasms', which is when we have a sexy dream, and even orgasm in our sleep. Sadly, the sensation often passes as soon as you open your eyes.

Our emotions can also have such a powerful effect on our pleasure that many sex therapists say our most sure-fire erogenous zone is our brain. We are turned on by what we see, smell, taste, touch – and imagine. For more on how women use their minds to climax, see Chapter 6.

'I have several different types of orgasm'

The following are descriptions by real women of their most intimate varieties of arousal.

'There are many different kinds of orgasm. Here are some I have: a warm, tingly feeling starting in my vagina and spreading through my tummy, thighs, breasts and the tips of my toes. Sometimes I have a feeling in my scalp that makes my hair stand on end; or an impossible glow that makes every pore of my body feel sensitive; or it's a tightness bursting into a warm glow and feeling of relaxation.'

Di

'A tingly feeling moves up my legs from my knees until it touches me between the legs. When it arrives I feel several large contractions, followed by small ones. Sometimes it is possible to go on to have another climax. This feels different, beginning with uncontrollable shaking, followed by the tingling up the legs.'

Nikki

'Sometimes they feel mind blowing: feelings of dizziness and floating overcome me and I feel warm and contented. Other times they feel very quick – a fast build-up and they're all over. Then other times the sensations are very mild, like fluttering.'

Jo

'My orgasms vary depending on whether I was stimulated orally, by intercourse or through masturbation. They're partly an emotional feeling, warm, sexy and pleasurable. Sometimes they make me feel giggly and squirmy. And I always want more. It's good to know that when it comes to this aspect of sex we have it all over men – we can have multiple orgasms.'

Scarlet

'With my last lover, I could climax just hearing his voice on the phone, but not when his penis was inside me.'

Della

➻ The female erection

At last science has accepted the existence of a female erection. You're probably having erections during sex – but the odds are you haven't noticed yet. An erection doesn't sound the sort of thing you can miss, but oddly enough we can, mainly because until recently women were discouraged from knowing anything about arousal or their own pleasure.

The word erection is also partly to blame. It makes you think of something that stands up in an obvious way – like a penis. For women, the outside effects of an erection are more subtle, but they're very real.

Here's how the erection begins: we think of sexual arousal starting in the body, but usually it begins with your largest sexual organ – your brain – where a sight, a sound or a smell sets off the signals of desire. In a woman, this translates very subtly into a physical reaction.

At first, she may just be aware of feeling a general sense of pleasure; she may also notice a warm sensation spreading through her lower belly. She's starting to become aware that she's aroused, but she might not be entirely sure. (It's easier for a man because it's at this stage that he might see the first stiffening of his penis.)

If stimulation continues, further changes happen. More blood rushes towards her genitals. The woman feels warmer and may find her clothes restricting as her muscles relax and swell. She may also develop a 'sex flush' on her face, neck and chest, and her pupils will dilate – these will be the only obvious signs of arousal. However her erection is already well under way.

Stimulation and arousal

As arousal increases, blood vessels in the shaft of the clitoris and the vagina swell and redden as they're filled by increased blood flow. It was once thought this happened to cushion the delicate female sexual organs from the impact of intercourse – this is one reason, but in fact the main one is to increase the woman's pleasure and give greater accessibility for the penis. The increased blood causes the outer lips to swell, become more defined and to part slightly at the entrance of the vagina, making it easier for the erect penis to enter.

So what becomes erect?

The answer is, the entire vaginal area, but particularly the clitoris, which acts in the same way as the penis. The clitoris head may look tiny but it's actually the tip of a complex system of nerve endings that lead back into your body and fan down your inner thighs. This is why some women notice their inner thighs can redden and swell slightly during sexual arousal. The part of the clitoris you see is merely the very tip of this enormous network of nerves.

The most sensitive section of these nerves is contained in a pencil-width bundle of muscles which curves up from inside the body, curling up above the clitoris in a U-bend, then ending in the clitoris itself. This bundle is known as the 'shaft' (much the same as the part of the penis below the head is known as the shaft). Because this shaft curls above the clitoris, a woman who doesn't enjoy direct stimulation to the clitoris may enjoy rubbing the area just above it. American sex researchers found that during sex most men stimulate the clitoris directly; however most women, while masturbating, move from direct stimulation to the sides and shaft of the clitoris as the head of the clitoris becomes too sensitive.

Exploring around the clitoris creates sensations similar to those experienced by a man when the shaft, rather than the head, of his penis is stimulated. This comparison makes sense because in many ways the vaginal area and clitoris is the same as the penis: it has the same amount of nerves, except they are spread out around the vagina, finishing in the clitoris, and in both cases the shaft of the sexual nerve complex is protected by a layer of tissue, thick enough to protect the nerves, but thin enough to allow a build-up of pleasurable friction.

Female ejaculation

The similarity doesn't end there; a man ejaculates at the point of orgasm, and scientists now recognise that some women do as well. For generations it was thought that woman couldn't ejaculate – that some women felt very wet after sex purely because they lubricated more than others.

To add to the confusion, some women also urinate slightly at orgasm, as a chain-reaction to the spasms caused around the uterus. Because the female bladder nestles just above the uterus, and the exit tube is very close to the vagina, waves of pleasure can cause a minor loss of control. Women can find this embarrassing, but in fact it's pretty common and just one of nature's little quirks.

However, some women stuck to their guns and said they felt an extra rush of wetness at the point of orgasm, and they were certain it wasn't urine. Sex researchers found they were right – they finally measured a liquid that wasn't lubricating fluid or urine: it was definitely a type of ejaculatory fluid. In fact the mixture produced by women is a blend of proteins and is similar to male seminal fluid, except it doesn't contain sperm.

Research continues into this fluid – as yet, no one knows which organ in a woman's body manufactures it, or if it has a special role to play during sex.

➡ Hormones and your sex drive

Have you noticed that sometimes you're so sexually charged you feel you're going to set the sheets on fire, yet other times you're happy to doze off with nothing more than a goodnight kiss? The reason for this is a mixture of things: emotions, tiredness, your relationship, and hormones.

The hormone with the greatest effect on your sexual cycle is oestrogen. Produced in the ovaries, oestrogen gradually builds up from day one of your menstrual cycle (the first day of your period) causing the endometrium (womb lining) to thicken and prepare for a baby. When the oestrogen reaches its highest point, between the eleventh and eighteenth days of your cycle, an egg is released from one of your ovaries and travels down one of the Fallopian tubes towards the uterus (or womb).

It's no coincidence that this is the time we feel the most horny and want to have sex. Nature has organised it so our brain and body are primed for action, maximising the chances of conception. The oestrogen's job isn't over yet, however. It also triggers a change in the mucus secreted from the cervix. Normally this mucus is made of little strands which criss-cross, but when you ovulate the mucus forms into thick parallel strands, forming pathways that help sperm swim up towards your cervix.

When you're feeling this keen for sex, it helps if your partner is too. If he isn't, try letting him smell your skin. This is because, when your oestrogen production peaks, your body also produces more of what are called 'social hormones' or pheromones. Contained in sweat and bodily excretions, they send subconscious 'turn-on' messages to the opposite sex. The amounts are so tiny that you can't actually smell a pheromone – it's just 'picked up'.

Pheromones also send out non-sexual messages – the synchronisation of monthly periods among women in all-female institutions is thought to be caused by pheromone messages drawing the women's body clocks together.

Exercise can also cause us to feel sexy. A toned and healthy body naturally makes us feel more confident, but exercise also pumps out sweat – and therefore more pheromones. This is one reason so many health clubs are romantic hunting grounds.

Funnily enough, although oestrogen is a major trigger for your sex drive, sometimes androsterone, one of the male hormones produced in a man's testes, can also get a woman's sex drive sparkling. Women's bodies naturally contain small amounts of so-called 'male hormones' such as androsterone and testosterone and these are thought to be linked to the sex drive. If a woman is suffering from a complete lack of sexual drive that has no apparent psychological reason, doctors sometimes administer a small dose of male hormones, which can put her body back in balance, and rev up her desires again.

Chapter 3

COUNTDOWN TO BLAST OFF

↔ Self-discovery quiz: who will you be compatible with in bed?

↔ What women wish men knew about the female orgasm

↔ Fine-tuning your foreplay – and how it can help you get what you want in bed

'I was madly attracted to this man once, but in bed it was a disaster. He wanted to go fast when I wanted to go slow, and he was being gentle when I wanted him to be forceful. Something just didn't click between us.'

Fiona

'I wish men would remember women aren't like lift buttons – pressing the clitoris harder does not send me to the top faster.'

Marie

➻ Self-discovery quiz

What's your sexual personality?

While most of us can identify the personality traits that make us successful at work, we know little about the mysterious forces that motivate us in moments of passion. It's a shame, as keying into your unique 'sexual personality' can give you an insight into what's important about your relationship – perhaps even what you'd like to adjust to make sex more exciting.

1. **If you had to describe your ideal love-making, you'd say . . .**

    D. Exciting and emotional, like something out of a film.
    B. No limits – lusty, maybe even kinky.
    C. I would like a man who makes passionate love to me and then allows me to bask in the afterglow in peace.
    A. Varied. I enjoy making love in new places.
    E. Tender and loving. Foreplay is crucial to me.

2. **How important is romance to you?**

    A. I like it. It adds spice to our relationship.
    D. Very. I love it when my partner brings me flowers. It's the ultimate expression of our love.
    C. It's pointless even trying to be romantic, mainly because it's not going to get through to my lover.

E.   It's nice sometimes, but it's not a prerequisite to good sex.

B.   Not very. I prefer passion.

3.   Do you find your partner attractive?

E.   Yes. He may not be a looker in other women's eyes, but I know the real him.

B.   Which one? I'm playing the field right now.

D.   Of course . . . although in a funny way he sometimes reminds me of my father.

A.   Definitely. Especially when he goes to work in his smart suit.

C.   I guess so. I haven't given it much thought.

4.   How much do you talk about sex?

B.   All the time. My friends love to hear about my sex life because it's so exciting.

A.   Quite a bit, especially with my lover. It's the best kind of foreplay.

C.   Hardly ever. It's a private thing.

E.   Now and then. Mainly, if something isn't right in our relationship we talk it out.

D.   Not as much as I'd like. My lover doesn't like it.

5.   How easy do you find it to ask for what you want in bed?

E.   Not too hard. I can usually tell him what I want but sometimes he needs reminding.

D.   It's difficult. I get embarrassed – what if he thinks I'm weird?

B.   It's easy. I give him directions.

C.   I don't really. There doesn't seem to be any point. I'm the only one who can really satisfy me.

A.   We talk a lot while we make love. It makes things more exciting.

6. Who usually initiates sex?

A.   He practically begs for it. I go along with it, but I prefer a little romance first.

C.   He does, most of the time.

D.   We take turns. He's good at sensing when I want him to take charge.

E.   We both do, generally, but if I'm too tired, he'll happily wait until morning.

B.   Often I do, but he's quick to follow my lead.

7. What did your parents teach you about sex?

C.   They felt strongly that it should be reserved for marriage.

E.   It can be exciting, dangerous and complicated if you're not careful. Treat it with respect.

A.   It's healthy and should be shared with Mr Right.

B.   I was always in trouble over it. My parents hated my boyfriends.

D.   My dad was often affectionate with me, sometimes at the expense of my mum.

8. In general, your parents . . .

E.   Are good. They've made mistakes, but we can usually work out our differences.

A.   Basically supported me 100 per cent.
B.   Are strict. They tried to control me when I was younger, especially when it came to boyfriends.
C.   Are distant. I always felt I had to try very hard to win their love.
D.   Are a pain. They just don't understand me.

9.   Your first sexual experience was . . .

C.   Quick, empty . . . and a bit scary.
D.   Embarrassing. I felt guilty afterwards.
A.   Enjoyable. I was lucky to have a generous boyfriend who boosted my confidence.
E.   So-so, but love-making improved as I became more comfortable with my sexuality.
B.   A total let-down. I just wanted to get it over and done with.

10.   How do you feel about your body during sex?

B.   I've got my not-so-good bits, like everyone else, but generally I feel okay about it.
A.   People tell me it's sexy.
C.   It has so many faults, I prefer not to look.
E.   It's okay, but I prefer not to display it when we're making love. I tell my partner where to touch me.
D.   Depends. Some days I can't stand to look in the mirror. Other days I think I look great.

HOW TO SCORE

You probably have a selection of several different letters, but you'll have chosen one more than the others. This is your uppermost sexual personality. If, for example, you have five 'A's, three 'E's, 1 'B' and 1 'C', read the answer headed Mostly 'A's: The Dynamo. You may also find it an insight to read your next highest score.

Mostly 'A's: The Dynamo

Lucky you! Boyfriends have been good to you. You've developed healthy sexual responses without guilt or anxiety. Your family has encouraged you in what you want to do, and chances are you've got a good body image and self-esteem most of the time.

A well-rounded sexual relationship is important to you. This is because you understand your body and enjoy sharing it – you're willing to explore sex just as you're willing to explore most other aspects of your life. This can make you bored and frustrated with Mr Missionary Position Only.

You'll also find it hard to feel satisfied with a man who has no career or drive. A man who's very laid back can make you feel tied-down, as can an inflexible or sexist man. If he has to be the boss or is shocked if you show any sexual appetite, he's not for you. You need a man who sees you as an equal.

Sometimes you lead in bed, sometimes he does. And although you're interested in commitment, you're by no means dull. Dynamos are always ready for sexual adventure. Happily, you're good at meeting men who relate to you as a person. Even if you do have some unhappy relationships, you'll eventually connect up successfully.

Mostly 'B's: The Go-Getter

Your friends sometimes call you wild and wonderful. You dress to please yourself but probably also to attract attention and you love the excitement of having a new man on the go. In bed, you are very assertive and have no problems letting men know exactly what it is you want. In this respect you are also very generous and like to make certain that your partner feels as fulfilled and satisfied as you do; that is you pride yourself on giving men their best sex ever. The likelihood is that you have also probably experimented freely with the wilder kinds of sex and like to take the lead. You are very comfortable with your own self-image, in particular your body, and feel completely at one with using it to give yourself and your partner pleasure.

When it comes to the men in your life, you like men who will respect you and will be as open and fun-loving when it comes to sex as you are yourself. In general you go for well-balanced men who like a lot of adventure and quite a few giggles. In this respect your background has probably helped you because, although strict, it has given you the confidence to pursue what you want.

In order to be happy, sexually or otherwise, you have to love yourself and be loved for you. This is something you probably learnt early in life and know how to put to good use.

Mostly 'C's: The Quiet One

You are quite a shy person and probably find the idea of sex slightly inhibiting. You enjoy it, but more often than not find it quite embarrassing and find it difficult to let go. Chances are you have some wonderful fantasies but for more sexual pleasure you have to speak up for yourself and let your partner know what it is you want from him. Try focusing on what *you* like during sex and ask for more of it. Little by little you will feel happier in bed, will grow in confidence and by doing so end up giving him more pleasure, too.

Trust is a key word for you. The type of man you would like to go out with is the type who will listen to you and draw you out of yourself. You may also enjoy masturbation so don't feel awkward about pleasing yourself. It's your body, you can do what you like.

The main thing to remember is that sex is supposed to be fun, so give yourself a chance to relax and enjoy it in its infinite variety. Talk to your partner about what will make you feel more comfortable about sex, experiment and learn to be at one with your body and yourself.

Mostly 'D's: The Romantic

You're a true lover of all things romantic and as such it is very important for you to look and act feminine and seductive. You probably like to buy nice perfumes and lingerie and love being showered with flowers. However, by focusing on how you appear to your partner it's easy to forget about your own desires. Give your lover the chance to focus on every inch of you.

Relax into the physical sensations. Don't dismiss new ideas and you'll soon find even more warmth in your lovemaking and even more freedom to be yourself.

While you love to captivate a man, you have the self-confidence to feel that you don't always need to follow through with sex. For you, romance, teasing and flirtations are just as fun as sex itself and you like a man who is as responsive and enjoys this side of a relationship as much as the physical side.

When it comes to your partners, you prefer men who have a definite career plan and who know where their lives are leading them. You are very generous by nature and have an enormously lively spirit and you like to see both these qualities reflected in the men you date.

Mostly 'E's: The Pragmatist

You're a complex woman with a combination of many sexual personalities, which only goes to show that you are not afraid to experiment and have some fun in the bedroom. You don't regret your past; it's taught you a lot about what makes you tick. You know relationships require work and you're willing to devote time to them so that you can reap ultimate satisfaction.

While sex is important to you, it doesn't dictate your life. Sometimes you dabble in the kinky, other times you enjoy conventional sex. For lovemaking to be enjoyable, you like a man who's prepared to show you he loves you and values you as a partner – in and out of bed.

You enjoy romance, but it's lower on your list of priorities than a man who delivers emotional support and respect. A relationship with a man who treats you badly won't last long.

Be careful you don't fall into a cosy rut sexually. It can feel ridiculous playing the sex-kitten or trying something risqué with a man you know very well, but think of it this way: sex is one of the glues that holds your relationship together. Isn't it worth strengthening that glue, especially if it's enjoyable at the same time?

⟶ What women wish men knew . . .

Here are some real women, talking about what men don't understand when it comes to women and orgasm.

'Most men think women have three erogenous zones: two nipples and a clitoris. So foreplay is playing with your breasts and rubbing between your legs. They forget the bottom, the neck, the back – the body attached to the genitals.'

Nadia

'Lubrication is 90 per cent of whether I orgasm or not. It doesn't matter if it's out of a tube from the chemist or from his mouth, as long as I'm wet during sex.'

Lisa

'Men think that what works for them will work for women. But softer works better than harder when it comes to the clitoris.'

Jane

'Lots of men think women's orgasms are chance occurrences beyond anyone's control. If only they'd take the time to get to know and understand our bodies better.'

Carolyn

'It's the clitoris that counts, not the vagina. Give the first enough attention and the second will respond.'

Emma

'Sex isn't a race. Slow down the pace sometimes. And when you think you've given her enough foreplay . . . give her some more.'

Rachel

'My idea of good foreplay is an orgasm orally or manually before intercourse.'

Lois

'Women can't shift gears as easily as men. We like to be emotionally ready before making love.'

Anna

➟ Fine-tuning your foreplay

Many couples spend the first few months together kissing and caressing, but once the initial dizzy lust has passed, those loving touches can evaporate. We can even start to feel embarrassed if we want to take time over foreplay – after all, men can be up and running sexually within minutes. So if it takes you half an hour or an hour to really warm up, you can start to feel just a tiny bit . . . selfish.

Well don't. The truth is, if you want to have more satisfying sex, foreplay is vital. Sure, we all enjoy the odd quickie now and again, but for long-term lust you need a slower approach most of the time.

The reason is the fundamental physiological response to sexual arousal. While the beginning of arousal is the same for both sexes – blood starts pumping faster around the body – the effects are hugely different. For men, the blood flow gets locked pretty quickly into the beginnings of an erection and they become aware of a very clear sensation focused in their penis. Given that the tip of the penis is packed with nerve endings, perhaps it's no surprise for many men that the next thing they want to do is physically stimulate the tip of that penis as fast as possible – in other words, get it inside you.

For women, the sensations that develop are much more diffuse. After causing the beginnings of vaginal lubrication the blood flow makes a woman's whole body (not just her vagina) more responsive to touch – stroking her inner thigh, her back or her hair can make her purr with pleasure. Scientific tests have shown that when it comes to skin sensitivity, the least sensitive woman is more sensitive than the most sensitive man. No one is sure whether this is purely physical, or psychological, because men are not encouraged to be in touch with their senses.

However, once you understand this difference in the speed of arousal, a lot of the sexual confusion between the sexes becomes clear. Many men assume women are aroused in the same way they are, so they pretty much head straight for the clitoris. Women, on the other hand, can't understand why their lover is 'bolting' through sex instead of lingering over her entire body. It can make you feel a bit rejected actually, as if he doesn't enjoy the sight of your body enough to take time over it.

'Foreplay is partly to get me aroused, but it's also a way of showing affection and passion. That's why it's important to me.'

Kerry

Giving him a hint

So how can you encourage a lover to give you the tender touching that you need? No one wants to think that they are lousy in bed, so before you launch a point-by-point critique of his foreplay, imagine how you'd feel if the tables were turned and you were being 'criticised'. In other words, kid gloves are needed for the best results.

Actions speak louder than words, so the advice most sex therapists give is to start off by trying to give him some guidelines by the way you respond to his touch. When he's doing something you enjoy, let him know by the way you move or the sounds you make.

'If he's rushing to get to "the good bit" I pull back and say something like, "Let's stroke each other." Or we try oral sex. If he does it right I really moan and groan and give him encouragement. Men pride themselves on being good lovers and once they see that you're getting more excited, they get more excited too.'

Jane

Other techniques include gently guiding his hand down or up, or whispering something encouraging in his ear like, 'That's amazing. Don't stop.' (Okay, it might not be amazing yet, but in the early days encouragement can only help.) If nothing else, he'll be thrilled to be doing the right thing, more aware of how you react and encouraged to get an even better reaction by trying something else.

'My boyfriend jokes that he's learnt everything about me from the "moan-o-meter". He'd tentatively place his hand somewhere and by how loud I moaned he'd know whether to stay there or move on.'

Suzanne

Setting the scene

Another way to minimise hurt feelings is to bring up the subject of foreplay in a non-sexual environment – that is, outside the bedroom. If you bring up your concerns immediately after sex – just when he's basking in a post-sex glow – he'll be too hurt and possibly angry to hear your point of view. Intimate dinners for two, cosy afternoons on the sofa, long walks in the park are all a much better bet.

'When I first started going out with my partner he'd only have sex in the missionary position. So one weekend we went to stay by the seaside. We went for romantic walks, held hands and had a really nice time. On the way back to the hotel I said, "It's so different here. Maybe we should try making love in a different way? What do you think?" He got the idea pretty quickly.

Afterwards he said he'd been wanting to try a few new things but was worried I'd be shocked.'

Julie

You can also try taking him to a film you know will be raunchy, or reading out a sexy passage from a novel, 'joking' that you'd like to try the techniques they describe some day. Perhaps describe a sexy dream you have had, which featured lots of foreplay – or ask him about his dreams. Who knows, he may have a few exciting suggestions of his own.

Great sexpectations

Opening up about your own vulnerabilities in bed can be a perfect way to open up a discussion.

'My boyfriend was very self-conscious about performing oral sex. He'd try and get it over as quickly as possible, which wasn't very satisfactory for me. So I said I felt awkward performing it on him and needed reassurance and help. Later he admitted he wouldn't mind a few tips from me. The sex is better and we're closer too.'

Tricia

Remember, keep telling him what you like, but be prepared to change what *you* do in bed: if you want him to fine-tune his foreplay, you'd best be prepared to fine-tune yours as well. If things take a little while to change, stay calm and revel in the thought that practice – lots of slow, juicy, exciting practice – will make perfect.

Foreplay favourites

Here are real women and men, confessing what turns them on:

'Making love with most of my clothes on, or very slowly being undressed by my lover. Keeping clothes on promises a lot, and slows things down.'

Paula

'Long, deep kissing. When I first met my boyfriend we'd spend hours kissing; now it's mostly hello and goodbye pecks.'

Kathy

'Having my partner come into the bedroom in a business suit, pretending that we're at my office. And then she seduces me.'

Mark

'Gently playing with each other – she touches my penis and I touch her clitoris. It's great not feeling rushed, just relaxing and taking your time.'

Brian

'Stripping for my partner.'

Tessa

'I love kissing the back of my partner's legs, because he finds it such a turn-on.'

Rachel

'Lying naked together and stroking each other.'

Clara

'A long massage with scented oils – but only when the room is warm as well. If I'm the least bit cold I just can't get into it.'

Jasmine

For more hints on foreplay tips that might work for you, see the sensate focusing exercises In Chapter 7.

Chapter 4

TRULY, MADLY, DEEPLY SEX

➨ Self-discovery quiz: are you in touch with your sexual desires – or could you be denying yourself peaks of pleasure?

➨ The passion/intimacy connection and how it leads to better orgasms

➨ Oral sex - the pleasures and techniques, including Do's and Don'ts

'I mostly have orgasms during sex only when I am on top. And I always have them during oral sex.'

Rita

'I've had six sexual partners but only had an orgasm with one of them. I think it might be because they've been mostly one-night stands where I prefer to give rather than receive. Hopefully the situation will improve with a long-term partner.'

Anna

❦ Self-discovery quiz

What's your pleasure potential?

Discover your orgasm potential with this quiz. Read the following questions and choose the answer that's closest to you. If you can't decide between two, choose both.

1. **If you sometimes have sex when you don't feel like it, what's the most likely reason?**

   ♥ You know that once you get going, you'll warm up and enjoy it.
   ❦ Your boyfriend wants to and you don't want to disappoint him.
   ❧ You always feel like having sex.
   ♦ You need some love and affection.

2. **For you, where does foreplay physically start?**

   ❦ When your breasts or genitals are touched.
   ❧ As soon as you know you are going to have sex you start feeling turned on.
   ♦ Once you begin kissing.
   ♥ With a back rub, holding hands, or other non-sexual contact.

3. **Getting more intimate, when do you masturbate?**

   ♦ Only when you're alone and won't be disturbed, like in the bath or bed.
   ❧ Either alone or in front of your partner – it turns you both on.

❦ You've only done it a few times, and you were alone.

♥ Usually alone, but sometimes with a partner to help you climax.

4. **Do you ever have orgasms in your sleep?**

♠ No, but sometimes you have dreams where you're having sex.

♥ You think you might have climaxed during erotic dreams, but you're not entirely sure.

❦ No, you don't think you ever have.

♣ Yes, definitely.

5. **Are your sexual fantasies . . .**

♥ Buried deep in your memory, but very real and physical once you conjure them up?

❦ Romantic and dreamy, with sex as the end of the scenario?

♠ Varied and sometimes you fantasise you're making love to someone else when you're with your partner?

♣ Always one or two thoughts away, and you can get very turned on thinking about them?

6. **Do you recognise if or when you actually need sex?**

♣ Yes, your body tells you.

♠ Kind of – you get really cranky and tense, then feel much better after making love.

❦ You don't think you ever actually need sex.

♥ Yes, you think you have needed it sometimes, but you don't have any signs you regularly recognise.

7. **Is an orgasm an all-over body experience for you?**

♥ Yes, after climaxing you tingle from head to toe.

♦ No, but you feel it very intensely in your genital area.

♣ Sometimes it feels like your whole body was involved, but you're not always sure it was an orgasm.

♠ Yes – and you can have an orgasm by touching your breasts or other parts of your body besides your genitals.

8. **How do you handle stress?**

♦ You get very stressed with work, friends and commitments and find it hard to switch off – a night out usually does the trick though.

♣ You allow yourself time to unwind alone, often listening to music or just relaxing.

♥ You have a hot bath and take time to really pamper your body.

♠ You go for a massage, facial or body treatment.

9. **How much do you and your partner discuss your sex life?**

♦ Not much. Never outside the bedroom.

♣ Never. You don't need to.

♠ You talk during sex, telling each other what feels good.

♥ You might initiate a quiet chat over a drink if you feel things aren't going too well.

10. When you become sexually involved with someone, which of the following sums up how you most regularly feel?

♥ Connected and content.
♥ Sensual and horny.
♥ Attractive and popular.
♣ Secretive and smug.

HOW TO SCORE

Mostly ♣

You occasionally climax when making love, so you're definitely orgasmic, but you could be enjoying the build-up far more and experiencing greater excitement with your partner. An orgasm is the icing on the cake for you, not part of the mix. You know how to get there, but sometimes you just can't (or can't be bothered?). You play it safe, only having sex when you really feel like it, possibly preferring the same route to pleasure every time. You're missing out on some great erotic opportunities. Why not let your partner persuade you to make love on the spur of the moment? Make him make you want him!

It's also worth remembering sexual pleasure doesn't have to start in the genital area. It's far more exciting to build an orgasm through contact with other parts of the body, so try thinking of (and using) your whole body during foreplay to boost your pleasure and confidence.

Try trusting your own sensations more – it can be easy to imagine other women's orgasms are more exciting than yours, which can leave you disappointed with your own. You may also find it hard to ask for what you want in bed because having desires is slightly embarrassing to you. Forget the images in your head of female film stars 'having orgasms' on the big screen. Real life isn't like that – you get sweaty and red-faced during sex – and that's before you've climaxed. Let yourself go; most men love this and your cellulite will be the last thing on their minds. Set time aside to explore your sensual side. This doesn't have to be masturbation. Why not pamper your body with luxurious creams and massages? You'll feel more in touch with your sensual side and this will intensify your sexual pleasure.

Mostly ♥

You're definitely orgasmic and you enjoy it to the max. Share your knowledge with your partner; if you know ways to get to an instant orgasm, show him. It might turn him on and will definitely help your communication with one another about your sexual needs. In-depth talking also boosts the intimacy in the relationship, which can lead to real mind-and-body orgasms. You probably already experience powerful climaxes that you can feel through your whole body, and this makes you feel very sensual and in control. This is wonderful, but at times you may be so sexually confident you're inflexible. You could be so into your climax you don't show much affection in bed. While it's wonderful to push back the sexual boundaries, your demands for excitement make you an intimidating partner – and can scare off someone who might take a little time to work up to revealing their inner fire. You may also find it difficult to stay excited in a long-term relationship, so you have concentrated on one-night stands or finished relationships when you thought the sexual spark had died. If you're unhappy in a relationship, despite the sexual fulfilment, examine your emotional needs – a relationship constantly needs working on.

Mostly ♥

Recognising how orgasmic you are has wonderful results in your relationships, but it could be even better, as there are certain times of the month when you're more orgasmic than others. Some sex therapists believe that pre-menstrual syndrome (PMS) is partly unreleased sexual energy, so before your period is a perfect time to explore your body's orgasmic potential and experience new highs. Also, try talking to your partner more in bed. You tend to reserve sex talk for when there's a problem, instead of emphasising the positive. Men love to be told when they're doing things right and how good it feels. Generally, however, you're an open and affectionate lover. You have few psychological hang-ups about sex, and love to experiment when you feel like it. For the question about sexual fantasies, you probably answered that yours are very real once you conjure them up. Why not share them with your partner? Your answers show your growing sexual confidence and mean you are ripe for new experiences. Explore this side of your personality and you could be in for a few wild surprises.

Mostly ❦

Like many women, you're probably not sure if you've had an orgasm. This is very common and nothing to panic about, as it's the pressure to have orgasms that often stops them. Remember that every woman and every orgasm is different – throughout this book you'll read many different descriptions from real women. Some describe their orgasms as intense, others say they are more quiet. Yet other women say they have different kinds of orgasm depending on what kind of sex they're having.

So, to find your own physical peaks of pleasure, try exploring your erogenous zones. Turn to Chapter 3 for tips on foreplay and Chapter 5 for tips on how real-life women masturbate, and why.

The fact is, 99 per cent of women are orgasmic: it just takes some longer to discover this. Some never do and still lead very happy lives. Your answers show you feel sexy and attracted to your partner, but find it hard to make the mind/body connection. You're also so busy trying to please him that your own pleasure often ends up on the back burner.

You're sensitive to your partner's moods and have sex when he wants to. You love the intimacy of a sexual relationship, but may have the notion that great sex is a 'natural' thing that happens automatically and if you haven't got 'it', well, tough. The truth is that sex is not separate from the rest of your life – and it requires the same thought, work and determination you give to the rest of your pleasures. Great sex takes time – and hot first-time romps can't sustain a long-term relationship; you also need trust, relaxation and courage. On the other hand, settling for a relationship with too few sexual thrills can lead to heartbreak later on. Sex has to be faced up to and the problems dealt with if it's to fulfil its potential for both partners. Once you're orgasmic, and recognise orgasms when they happen, you'll be on the way to the sex life of your dreams.

➤➤   The passion/intimacy connection

Being intimate means you trust each other enough to share your secret desires and it can lead to better orgasms . . .

'The sex I have with my current boyfriend is the best I've ever had. It's different with him because we trust each other. I know he loves me so I feel comfortable, even if we get a bit kinky. On a one-night stand I never felt relaxed enough to suggest things I liked, so I didn't have orgasms as often.'

Lisa

When it comes to sex with a long-term partner, women tend to split into two camps – those who think it makes sex better, and those who think it makes sex less exciting. Certainly, in movies hot sex is generally portrayed as happening to people who've just met.

'Love and sex are incompatible. The best sex going is sex with strangers, silent sex or sex with someone who doesn't speak your native language.'

Juliette

In contrast, sex in a long-term relationship is seen as cosy, comfortable, safe . . . and a bit boring. It doesn't have to be this way. The closeness you have in an intimate relationship, when your lover is your best friend and he's there for you night and day, can help you create the most exciting sex of all.

The big difference is that when you're with a new lover you tend to censor yourself. It shows itself in silly little ways, like not making too much noise in bed in case he thinks you're unfeminine, or in big ways, like not suggesting new positions, in case he gets frightened by your experience or enthusiasm in bed.

True intimacy allows you to express yourself – and take risks in bed. Always secretly fancied having your hands tied together with silk scarves during sex? Now's your chance. Love the idea of being massaged for an hour before sex? A long-term boyfriend's the one to ask. Says Becky, 'Tom and I totally accept each other. We can be as sleazy or imaginative as we like in bed because neither of us feels the other will run a mile. This means we can discuss what we want. It takes us to a deeper level. We just get wilder and wilder in bed every year.'

The pleasure you get from sex together can also make the rest of your relationship more enjoyable. Rebecca describes how she felt about her sex life before she met her current partner: 'I was getting enough sex from short-term relationships. It was human contact, but in the majority of cases it left me feeling a bit cold. If it went badly I felt more alone than if I hadn't interacted with a guy at all. I wanted to be making love with all of my organs, including my heart and my brain, not just the ones between my legs.'

Certainly, sex experts agree that the more you know about someone, the more you can discover about what turns them on in bed. You find out how their minds work, the secret places they like to be touched, the teasing they prefer. This means you can start to use your imagination to build on what you already know about each other. Perhaps you remember that he got excited when you grabbed him unexpectedly . . . so you try something similar, but wIth a new twist.

Similarly, the familiarity of his touch, look and smell is important. Experts particularly rate smell as one of the most important physical links in human relationships – we may not notice it consciously, but our sense of smell makes us feel very connected and comforted. Tests show that, faced with a pile of identical T-shirts worn by strangers, lovers can nearly always pick out the one worn by their own partner, purely by the faint smell left on the fabric.

Intimacy also has a positive effect on the other relationships in your life – with your friends, family and at work. In an intimate relationship you're no longer sailing against the tide of life alone. You've got someone to help navigate when you feel you're losing direction, and to help bail out when conditions get stormy. Most of all, you have the self-confidence that comes from revealing your personality – dark side, temper and all – and knowing you're still loved. That can be the sexiest thing in the world.

❧ What we love about sex

This is what some real women said:

'I don't see sex as an emotional thing. It's purely physical and pleasure oriented. I love the actual mechanics of sex, especially when he first goes in and we're in the missionary position. You can say what you like about the *Kama-sutra* but the tried and tested positions are the best.'

Sharon

'I enjoy just about everything about sex, even the embarrassing bits like making weird noises and taking your clothes off in front of someone for the first time. The ultimate has to be sex with someone you love; the feelings go deeper and it really means something.'

Louise

'I love having my feet played with, and being kissed on the back of the neck makes me go all dreamy. Sex is great in the afternoon, particularly when you're not expecting it. But you can't beat the sex you have with someone you've just met – there's a lot to be said for pure lust.'

Mandy

'I'm a cuddle person. I love the cuddling that goes on before, during and after sex. Affectionate sex after a hard day at work leaves me less stressed. It beats going to the gym every time.'

Joanne

'I love the anticipation beforehand, being kissed slowly is a real turn-on, the foreplay, the sexy games and the actual shebang. Nothing is better than the powerful floating feeling you get after an orgasm.'

Marie

'I am a romantic and I love the feeling of being so close to someone that there is no space between us, physically or mentally – almost to the point that you're so wrapped up in each other that you forget about the rest of the world. This kind of sex is rare, but it's unforgettable.'

Anna

'I love the way the closeness and pleasure seem to put all other things in perspective. No matter how stressed I am, sex lifts my spirits and makes me realise that, actually, life isn't so bad after all.'

Tess

'My most sensitive erogenous zones are in the upper part of my body. I love to be touched all around my neck, shoulders and face. Sex is much nicer with someone you really fancy, because you're always anticipating it and you're constantly turned on.'

Jean

'I love to make a whole meal out of sex. When you have the time to spend in bed together, sex becomes the hors d'oeuvre for the rest of the day. I like to work up a huge appetite so I can make scrambled eggs and take them, croissants and coffee back to the bedroom. That way you can luxuriate together for the rest of the day.'

Julie

'I love being talked dirty to, especially during foreplay, which is usually much better than the actual sex. Another turn-on is being touched or kissed lightly on my nipples or bottom.'

Emma

↔ Oral sex

The pleasures and the techniques

Oral sex is what you might call a sticky subject. Some women enjoy using their mouth on their partner, others do it grudgingly, and some don't do it at all. We can also have mixed feelings about his mouth on our vagina – instead of losing ourselves in the pleasure we can find ourselves wondering if he's doing it out of a sense of duty. Is he bored? Does he hate the smell and taste? Is this a bit too intimate? However, if you can relax and enjoy it, you may find, like many women, that oral sex almost guarantees orgasm. Here are just a few of the enthusiastic descriptions from *Company* magazine readers:

'Tongue stimulation is good for me. Penetrative sex is more of a disappointment as I feel it's me giving pleasure more than receiving it.'

Denise

'I rarely come through penetration, but I love wrapping my legs around my partner's head when he is licking or teasing me through oral sex.'

Jo

'Oral sex is my favourite way to come. He can tease you for a while, by licking nearby, then the feel of his warm tongue on my clitoris is wonderful. Also, I get turned on by the fact that it's his mouth on my most intimate parts.'

Sharon

'I always have an orgasm through masturbation or oral sex – which is my favourite because the feeling of a warm, wet tongue is amazing, and because it gives the perfect pressure. Sex is best for me when I start with an orgasm through oral sex, then we make love and he has his orgasm.'

Janet

'Sometimes we both agree to have oral sex; that way we can get maximum pleasure. It's best if I lie on my back with him between my legs. That way I can writhe about, bend my legs, arch my back and grab on to things when I come.'

Grace

It can also be equally exciting to pleasure your partner through oral sex. 'It makes me feel very feminine,' said one reader. 'It's my thing. I enjoy it and I can tell from their reaction that I do it well. That makes me feel very powerful.' However, you do not have to be 'an expert' to enjoy (or be good at) oral sex. Most men say that the mere fact that you are performing it on them is so thrilling that the details are often lost in the blur of it all.

One common worry for women is how to cope with the man's ejaculation. If you want him to come in your mouth, think first what you are going to do with the fluid – you basically have two choices: swallowing or discreetly spitting into a tissue. If you're not keen on him coming in your mouth, don't worry that you'll spoil his pleasure – you can merely pull back at the crucial moment and use a wet hand to finish him off. One man advises, 'Just don't leave the guy flailing away like a rogue fire hose. That makes you feel she hates the whole thing.' He also said, 'She can pull back and let you come over her body . . . that's good too.' The point is: when it comes to oral sex, do only what you enjoy. There is no law that says you have to like oral sex, so if it's not your scene, don't feel obliged. Says one reader, 'I don't mind doing it, but I'm not mad about it because it feels one-sided.'

Do's and Don'ts for him

- Do perform oral sex because you want to, not because you think it's expected. She'll get the hint you're not enjoying it.
- Do ask what she likes – preferences vary from woman to woman.
- Do start out slowly and gradually – kiss the stomach and stroke the inner thigh, working up to the vagina.
- Do use your lips and tip of the tongue loosely at first, licking the area moist.
- Do, when her excitement grows, concentrate on the clitoris with the tip of your tongue – flick back and forth with your tongue, press down on the clitoris, suck hard or gently . . . try them all and see which ones your partner prefers.

- Don't just bury yourself under the bedclothes. Find a position that is satisfying for both of you – you may want eye contact or to hold hands.
- Don't stop caressing the rest of her body – the light touch of your fingers on other sensitive areas can increase arousal.
- Don't blow into the vagina, especially if the woman

is pregnant. This could cause a fatal air embolism of the brain.

- Don't wonder if she's really enjoying it – just take time afterwards, or the next day, to ask for suggestions on anything you could be doing differently.

Do's and Don'ts for her

- Do kiss, caress and touch his balls – they are very sensitive.
- Do remember you can use your hands at the same time – to start him off, or control his movements (a gentle but firm grip at the base of his penis can prevent him moving too deeply into your mouth).
- Do put pressure on the stem of the penis, softly drawing back the foreskin.
- Do make your mouth 'hollow' and flick your tongue against his penis on the in and out strokes.
- Do pay attention to other sensitive parts – hip bones, backs of knees, his bottom and the area between his balls and anus.
- Do follow your instincts. If you pay attention to your partner's reactions you'll soon discover what turns him on the most.

- Don't pull back the foreskin roughly.
- Don't knock or roughly squeeze the balls.
- Don't bite the head of the penis.
- Don't ram your tongue into the opening at the tip.
- Don't feel obliged to try and take the entire penis into your throat; you risk gagging.

Chapter 5

ME, MYSELF AND I

➦ Real women talk candidly about the joy of masturbation – and the guilt

➦ How to discover your hidden pleasure zones, including the G Spot and the A Spot

'I don't want to have sex with every Tom, Dick or Harry, but I do want to have orgasms. So I use my fingers on my clitoris and always bring myself off. To start I get myself horny by reading an explicit book. It takes a good fifteen minutes before I feel myself coming. Sometimes I play with myself again and have another.'

Jayne

'DIY with your own hand is a guaranteed route to orgasm. I know where to go and what to do. And if you have a sexual partner and you don't feel inhibited, you can show him exactly what you like. I find this really helps.'

Scarlet

●+ Masturbation – the how, the why and the guilt

Sometimes you just can't win. If you admit you masturbate, some people still see you as a sex fiend – and if you don't, people decide you're a prude.

Well, it's finally time to be honest. Research suggests that not only do most women masturbate (up to 82 per cent), many say it's a vital part of their sex life, just as important – if not more so – than intercourse with a man. After all, how can you tell a man how you like to be touched, if you've never touched yourself?

'Masturbation has a lot to recommend it,' explains sex expert and relationship therapist Dr Alan Riley. 'Being comfortable with your sexuality definitely leads to personal contentment. Feeling that your needs are abnormal and suppressing your sexual urges can lead to major psychological hang-ups.' He adds that masturbation helps you feel good about your body; frees you from the feeling that the only real road to sexual pleasure for a woman is a man; and it gives you orgasms, something that vaginal penetration doesn't always do.

But enough from the experts – here's what real women have to say:

'I can't remember when I learnt to masturbate, but I do remember when I was little I used to lie on top of my teddy bear because the hardness of his nose between my legs was amazing. Now, when I masturbate I make sure I have an orgasm every time. It helps me know myself. The most amazing times are when you know there's no going back – you've stimulated yourself to the point that nothing else matters. There are a lot of things about myself I don't like but I can be proud of one thing – I give myself the best damn orgasms this side of the Atlantic.'

Anna

'For me it's impossible to achieve an orgasm with a man thrusting in and out. That doesn't mean I don't enjoy making love. I do, but it's more because of the desire involved. I just cannot achieve an orgasm without clitoral stimulation . . . so I try to touch myself as we make love.'

Joanna

'Until I was twenty-one I thought I had orgasms. Then when I was washing myself using a shower attachment I felt an incredibly pleasurable sensation when the water pressure touched my clitoris. Although the pleasure was nearly unbearable, I kept moving the water on and off and this finished in an explosive experience that left me in no doubt what I had experienced. Since then I've never had any trouble reaching an orgasm through masturbation – it's taught me the incredible pleasure I'm capable of feeling.'

Nikki

'I've been masturbating from a young age – ever since I discovered a warm feeling sliding down my nan's banister. I climax more often when I masturbate by myself than during sex. I always do it the same way, using the edge of the duvet.'

Candy

Mixed feelings

As an added bonus, scientists have discovered that orgasms – however you get them – can lessen stress (women's ability to bear pain increases by over 200 per cent just after climaxing), plus they relax period pains and help prevent vaginal atrophy (thinning, drying and loss of elasticity in the walls of the vagina and around the vulva). They theorise that the lubricants produced during sexual activity keep the vagina moist and healthy.

So, if masturbation feels so good and it's healthy, why do we so often have mixed feelings about it? We may enjoy it, and know it helps us learn about what our body enjoys, yet sometimes we still feel guilty or embarrassed. Says Denise, 'I only started masturbating this year. I thought it was dirty before. Often I combine it with thinking about my lover, or things I've read in books.' Perhaps it's because masturbation is something you do for yourself – and women are often taught to put other people first, even in bed. Says Di, 'I love to masturbate while making love, but when I'm making love for the first time with a new man I wouldn't masturbate in front of him. I don't want this kind of intimacy early on – and it can intimidate some men.'

Another *Company* magazine reader, Lucy, adds: 'Sometimes you're not in the mood to share your body with anyone else, and it can be nice to just do something for yourself. But I sometimes feel guilty afterwards, like I've been caught with my hand in the biscuit jar.'

If the way you were brought up was very strict it can also be hard to enjoy masturbation without guilt. 'Because of my upbringing masturbation is a sinful taboo,' says Stephanie. 'I feel guilty that I do it and fear people can see tell-tale signs of my sexual activity on my face. Even so I masturbate whenever I feel pressured or lonely. I don't use my hands, I just press my thighs together and the feeling comes.'

What if you don't think of masturbation as a sin, but sometimes find it boring or unsatisfying? Is there something wrong with you? The short answer is No. Jayne speaks for many of us when she says, 'I can sometimes masturbate for a long time and not climax – for example, if I'm worried or tired. It annoys me then.' – You may just not be especially keen on the sensations. Says Lauren, 'I can go for months without masturbating. Then I feel like it and do it twice in one night. I can't say what turns me on exactly. It's just not that big a deal to me.' Fine, if you're happy, there's no problem. However, if you wonder if you could be having more enjoyable orgasms, more frequently, you can try varying your methods of masturbation.

Although every woman is an individual, which means we all have our own special ways of masturbating, sex researchers have discovered several trends. The Hite Report, compiled by American sex researcher Shere Hite, who interviewed 3,000 women, found 73 per cent of women tend to masturbate lying on their backs.

'I lie on my back and touch myself very gently and slowly with my forefinger. Perhaps the best time is when I masturbate with my lover helping me, pushing his fingers into me and touching my bottom.'

Di

Most said they masturbated every week or every couple of weeks, but added that it partly depended on whether they were in a sexually satisfying relationship, or on their emotional state, or even on how much privacy and free time they had.

It's also common for women to use fantasy when they masturbate. (For more on this, see Chapter 6.) These fantasies don't have to be complicated to be effective, as letters from *Company* magazine readers show. Says Delia, 'My fantasies are about past episodes with real lovers. Sometimes I also remember sexy scenes from films.' Adds Rachel, 'Sometimes I pretend I'm with a childhood sweetheart, who I only got to kiss in real life. Other times I imagine I'm with a complete stranger who finds me incredibly sexy.'

Anna wrote, 'My imagination plays a large part in my sex life – fantasies are a perfect way to let my mind wander into an erotic world which I don't have the nerve to enter physically. A few years ago I was an au pair in Israel. I was on a beach one day and got talking to a guy, who suddenly pulled me under the boardwalk and started kissing me – it was the first kiss I ever felt in my groin. His hands never went below my waist but I could tell how excited he was. Then he gave me his phone number – but I never called. At night sometimes I get turned on by re-enacting the whole event in my mind, using my own hands on myself. It has all the perfect ingredients for a fantasy. I was in a hot, exotic country with a stranger and I had control because I had his number. Even now, years later, I can still feel him against me.'

➼ Discover your hidden pleasure zones

If you find masturbation unsatisfying, or wish to get even more pleasure from your private sessions, sex therapists recommend experimenting with different methods. You could try the following:

- Make yourself comfortable in a warm room where you know you won't be disturbed. Light a candle if you like, or put on some relaxing music, but don't create a situation that seems unnatural to you or you'll feel self-conscious. After a warm bath or shower is good, as you'll naturally feel warm and relaxed, plus you'll be naked.

- Stand in front of the mirror. Pay attention to the whole of your naked body. Admire yourself, concentrating on the parts you like best.

- Take some oil or talc and rub it gently on your hands. Massage your neck, using both hands, knead your shoulders and neck and feel your tension draining away.

- Run your fingers down over your breasts (especially the nipples), over your arms, stomach and down your thighs. Reach around and caress as much of your back and bottom as you can. Feel the reaction to your own touch – where feels best?

- Vary the kind of touch you use – do soft, feathery touches feel better, or firm strokes? Try not to think about anything else.

- Caress your inner thighs and knees, gradually working up to the outer lips of your vagina. If you are excited by the sight of yourself, position a mirror in front of you. However, many women prefer to close their eyes and lose themselves in a fantasy.

- Try exploring your clitoris, but if it feels too sensitive, explore around and about the area; the skin above the clitoris can be particularly sensitive for many women.

- Some women find they can reach orgasm more quickly by lying on their stomachs. Experiment with your own position, noticing the different sensations every time you move.

- Don't get impatient with yourself. Like the rest of sex, masturbation to orgasm can take practice. You may need more than one session to find what turns you on.

- Vibrators are highly recommended by sex therapists for women who have difficulty reaching orgasm – or you can cheat and use a battery-powered massager, available from the chemist. Although many vibrators come in the shape of a penis, researchers have found it's the vibrations that trigger orgasm in women, not the penis shape. That's why over 90 per cent of women who use vibrators do not insert them into their vagina – instead they hold it against the skin near the clitoris (placing it on the clitoris itself can be too intense and painful). Says Joanna, 'With a vibrator I can have orgasm after orgasm – but I must wait a minute between them otherwise my clitoris is too sensitive. The area I stimulate is also different each time – never on the clitoris but slightly to the side, above or below.'

To stimulate your G Spot

Wet your fingers and gently slide them up the front wall of your vagina (the side nearest your stomach). About two inches up you will feel a small mass of spongy tissue about the size of a 50-pence piece. Stroke it gently and you will feel the tissue harden and swell with pleasure.

To stimulate your A Spot

Continue running your fingers up to the cervix at the back of the vagina. The cervix feels like a firm but mobile lump, rather like the end of your nose. Midway between your cervix and your G Spot you'll find an area that's smooth and extremely sensitive to the touch – that's your A Spot. Slide a finger up and down, using the G Spot as your boundary.

Chapter 6

MIND GAMES AND FANTASIES

➤ Real women confess what turns them on mentally

➤ Your sexual dreams – and what they can tell you about your sexual relationship

➤ Fantasising about other women

➤ Men's fantasies – and how we fit in

'I don't use fantasies if I'm with a partner as my arousal is already happening physically, but if I'm masturbating I think of fantasies, usually sexy films I've seen, and that can be enough to arouse me. Other times, I "talk dirty" to my partner or we re-live the most exciting or different past sexual encounters we've had with one another.'

Mandy

'There wouldn't be so much sexual pleasure without fantasies so I use them a lot – I think we should all be more sexually imaginative to make sex the best fun for both of you.'

Suzie

⟶ Real women confess what turns them on

It is common for a woman to use fantasies while masturbating or while having sex. It doesn't necessarily mean her real-life partner is not exciting enough – or that she wants her fantasies to come true. Basically, they are just no-strings-attached, guilt-free fun. Here's how some real women describe their own special fantasies.

'My favourite fantasy is being an exhibitionist – which I'm not in real life as I'm very self-conscious about my body. In my fantasy I'm on the train going to work when a gorgeous male stranger gets on. We flirt, kiss and before I know it he's performing oral sex on me. The train is crowded but I don't care and I carry on screaming out in sheer ecstasy. He makes me come, kisses me, then gets out at the next station, leaving me glowing and satisfied. Sometimes in my fantasy I can't come and everyone in the entire train carriage gives me oral sex until I am satisfied.'

Jo

'I have sexual fantasies during sex with my partner. They can be anything from fantasising about lesbian sex to sex with other people or pretending I've been "bought" (like I'm playing a prostitute or the wife of someone very old and rich).'

Rita

'Generally I orgasm when I have sex, but my fail-safe method is one particular fantasy. Without going into details, a four-poster bed inspired me . . . '

Sharon

'I haven't had many orgasms and they make me feel so vulnerable that I cry afterwards, which I feel spoils the moment. So I fantasise about having the most energetic and elaborate orgasms, without the tears, and this is enough for me now.'

Leane

'I use fantasies to get me excited. Sometimes I imagine I'm someone from a TV series, from fiction, even a cartoon character. Then I think up exciting situations that can happen to this character.'

Stephanie

'I don't really like porn films. I've seen a few and found them boring, but when I'm having sex sometimes I think about sexy scenes in ordinary films. I imagine the leading man desires me, and is looking at me with lust, like he does on screen. At the moment I've got a thing about Ralph Fiennes, but it was Keanu Reeves and Dennis Quaid before him. It's not so much the actor for me, it's the role he plays and whether he's sexy in that role.'

Katherine

'I imagine that I walk into a party and I am easily the most gorgeous woman there. Every man is panting for me, pressing up against me with erections. In real life this wouldn't happen because I am just an ordinary person and feel shy most of the time, but in my fantasy I am sexy, selfish and I can have any man I want. In the end we have the most enormous orgy on the floor, with men's cocks coming at me from all angles, fighting to satisfy me. I do everything – oral sex, anal sex, you name it. It feels very wicked, and turns me on so much.'

Lucy

'My favourite fantasy is really simple. I can't understand the elaborate ones some women have. I just fantasise about having very horny, passionate sex. He sees me, rips my clothes off and we're fucking like maniacs. That's it. No lead up, no elaborate story. Just raw sex. Great!'

Justine

➻ Serious, silly or shocking – your sexual dreams

Our sexual dreams can fascinate, delight or embarrass us. They can even be shocking or frightening. Dreams can remind us of our best sexual experiences – or remind us of what we're missing. They can tell you exactly what you need to know about yourself and your relationships at the time you most need to know – right now.

Our dreaming brain responds as quickly to relationship distress as the fire brigade does to a fire. For example, if you dream your new lover is smothering you with a pillow, it may be a valuable tip-off that deep down, you suspect he wants to smother you in the relationship.

Your erotic dreams may focus on actual sex acts, or deal with the emotional aspects of your relationship. Take Zoe's dream about a vampire: 'He's seducing me . . . but I know what I'm getting myself into. He even shows me his fangs. In my dream I have a daughter [in real life, she has no children] and I want to protect her. I'm screaming "No!" but I can't be heard and I feel horrified at myself for letting him sink his fangs into me.'

In her dream Zoe wanted to lose control and was terrified of it at the same time. In real life she was going out with a man she knew did not love her. Although she didn't love him either, she thought she could handle such a casual relationship. As it turned out, she ignored her dream and failed to protect her vulnerable side (her dream daughter).

The picture symbols we see in our dreams can be confusing to our waking minds. An upsetting dream about having sex without a condom doesn't necessarily mean you fear getting pregnant – it may show that you fear rushing into a relationship too fast, without protecting your heart. Dreaming of having sex with family members can make you feel guilty when you wake, especially if the dream sex is pleasant. (When incest survivors dream of sex with family members the sex is often unpleasant.) However, this dream doesn't mean you secretly yearn to have sex with someone in your family – it may represent a desire for emotional closeness, or a desire to be more like that person, if they have qualities you admire.

Danger signs

When the spark goes out of a relationship it's often hard to put your finger on why, but your dreams can give you insights. Says Shelly, 'I was bored in bed – and with the relationship. I kept blaming him for it. But then I had a dream where I was lying in bed wearing frumpy clothes. When I woke up I realised I was partly to blame for our dull sex life – I'd just completely stopped trying.'

You can even call up these dream insights by deliberately asking yourself questions – like 'Why am I so bored?' – just before you go to sleep. Rachel did this after months of feeling increasingly confused by her boyfriend's on/off interest in her: 'I dreamt that four men I know invited me over to have sex with them. I accepted and we had great sex together. Then one of the guys who had phoned criticised me and said I was too forward. I got angry and said "Hey, didn't you invite me over to have sex in the first place? Make your mind up."' When she woke Rachel realised the dream pointed out something she'd missed. Her boyfriend had a strong double standard about sex. He encouraged her to have wild sex with him, but afterwards he was very withdrawn. Her dream wasn't about some hidden desire on her part to have sex with four men – it symbolised her desire to feel more daring in bed and more accepted out of it.

Dreams in which you or your lover are unfaithful can make you feel very threatened – but they can be symbols of your emotional life. Eve had this dream: 'I realise Charles has been having an affair with this mousy, clinging woman. I'm furious and say he has to pay more attention to me, but he says the other woman needs him so much he can't deny her.' Eve realised the mousy woman was the clingy side of herself. 'The mature, sexy side of me is furious because I have encouraged Charles to pay so much attention to her that our sex life is suffering.'

If it's you having the fling in your dream, concentrate on how you feel when you wake; are you sad at having missed the opportunity, or relieved? Either feeling can give you an insight into your real-life relationship. If in your dream you go ahead with your infidelity, and have great sex, think how you could incorporate some of the things you did into your real sex life.

➻   When you fantasise about other women

It is estimated that up to 90 per cent of women in Britain have fantasised about sex with another woman. However, sex therapists point out that, although all of us are bisexual (capable of feeling attracted to both sexes) to some extent, this doesn't mean all of us secretly long to have sex with women in real life.

Sometimes a lesbian fantasy is just a convenient way of turning yourself on and feeling particularly free and wild.

'In real life I only have eyes for my boyfriend, but sometimes during sex I fantasise that women I admire and dream of being like are having a threesome with my boyfriend and me. That really turns me on.'

Sasha

'I fantasise but not during sex. I use it when I masturbate as I can think all sorts and no one gets hurt. My favourite is sex with another woman – I get really turned on. Or I imagine a threesome with another woman and a man. But I never fantasise about people I know as I'd feel silly talking to them later. Created characters work better for me.'

Grace

'Here's a favourite fantasy of mine: I'm having trouble reaching orgasm with my new boyfriend, so he invites two girls into the bedroom. They start exploring each other's bodies, licking and sucking each other's breasts and performing oral sex on each other. Then they start stroking me too. My boyfriend now has a hard-on and we all end up in an orgy.'

Jane

⇥ Men's sexual fantasies

The most common sexual fantasy men have is sex with their regular partner but in a different location or new position. Statistics are hard to find, but according to some studies, at least 40 per cent of men fantasise regularly during sex. Some men say they don't bother fantasising then because they have enough stimulation already – but 99 per cent admit to enjoying fantasies during masturbation.

An active fantasy life doesn't necessarily mean a man is unhappy with his sex life. On the contrary, fantasy is just part of an active sex drive – a sign that his sexual engine is humming along in top gear. Men don't fantasise because they're bored, or because they're not getting enough sex. They do it because they like it.

'There's no evidence that men's fantasies about other women increase with the duration of a relation-ship,' explains sex therapist Dr Alan Riley. 'Couples can get bored – but not with each other. They get bored with the sexual routine, sex in the same position at the same time and in the same place.'

Men don't necessarily want their sexual fantasies to come true either – he may have a favourite fantasy about an orgy but have no desire in real life to have sex with strangers. It's just a no-strings-attached turn-on.

If you're tempted to discover his fantasies, take care – he may want to keep them private. Experts say the best way to discover his dreams is to share your own and see how he reacts. Perhaps you've always liked the idea of making love in front of a roaring fire – try telling him and see how he reacts. Dianne follows this method: 'Generally, when I'm with my lover, we share our fantasies by talking. We also "lend" each other fantasies for masturbating – it can be sex with strangers, spanking, bondage, anything. I also fantasise about things my partner and I haven't done yet – or things we've done and really enjoyed. I know he does too.'

Four common male fantasies

Broadly speaking, researchers divide men's sexual fantasies into four separate categories:

Intimate. The most common of all. He imagines sex with someone he feels affection for, but in an unusual place – for example, he might dream about having sex with you outdoors instead of in the bedroom.

Exploratory. He imagines his lover or himself in very unusual situations or trying new techniques – taking part in an orgy, for example.

Impersonal. The woman is no one he knows – she's just an imaginary sex partner who'll do whatever he wants. Men who have a fetish – which means they are turned on only by certain clothes or objects – come into this category. A true fetishist is turned on by the object, rather than the woman. If he has a fetish for leather shorts, for example, it doesn't matter who's wearing them.

Sado-masochistic. Not necessarily involving real pain. Men are more likely to imagine that a woman they desire is lovingly teasing them to distraction before sex rather than actually hurting them.

Chapter 7

GUARANTEED JOY

◆◆ The ten most exciting sexual positions for women

◆◆ How to have a vaginal orgasm

◆◆ Seven steps to joygasmic sex. They'll make your sex life better – really, really better

◆◆ The total-body orgasm – discover the techniques sex therapists use to help women feel more pleasure

'A favourite position for me is lying on my back with my legs on his shoulders – but the doggie position is the best of all in my opinion.'

Candy

'My first dead cert for an orgasm is using a vibrator. Second comes oral sex, next comes sitting astride my partner on a chair or sofa. But I can enjoy so many positions, with the right mental attitude.'

Rachel

◂▸ The sexual positions women love the most

You wonder, don't you, just who exactly tries those positions in sex manuals. Often the pictures look so complicated you suspect you have to be a gymnast to do them.

That's why we asked three real-life couples, all in their twenties, to test ten of the most exciting sexual positions for women. Couple A are Justine and Mark, couple B are Fiona and Bradley, and couple C are Mark and Roz.

Their insights will give you much more information than the standard sex manuals.

1. Queen of the Castle

Woman sitting upright, astride reclining man

Pleasure Points: 10/10

Couple A

Her: This is great! It's a turn-on to see the pleasure you can give your partner – plus there's a good chance you can orgasm yourself.

Him: Great! It's best of all when you take it in turns to be active or passive, otherwise the man can feel a bit left out.

Couple B

Her: You can move freely in lots of directions, and because you can control the sensations, you can feel

Queen of the Castle

explosive sensations, or take it gently and prolong the pleasure.

Him: I love to see my partner moving on top of me and being turned on. It's very exciting. Plus you're free to stroke her breasts, hips and stomach. All in all, a treat.

Couple C

Her: In this position I felt waves of pleasure right up my spine. When I'm arched over my partner, it's even better.

Him: It's magic. Especially when she swings her pelvis backwards and forwards, her breasts look so wonderful.

Is it for you? Many women say this is the position that most guarantees them orgasm. Ideal if you aren't keen on strong penetration, but you need a strong back to swing your pelvis up and down and from side to side, otherwise it can lack physical sensations. It's a very visual position so for real sexual fireworks, don't do it in the dark – light a candle and really look into each other's eyes.

Variations: You can lean forward on your lover's chest or backwards, but in this position forceful movement can irritate the penis, so go slowly.

2. Spoons

Partners lie on their sides, penetration takes place from behind

Pleasure Points: 9/10

Couple A

Her: Everything happens gently, but there's deep penetration. It's great to feel completely cuddled by your partner and you can just lie there and let things take their course.

Him: This is the most 'together' position, as you touch all up and down your bodies. And the man has a comfortable grip, so he can easily control the movement.

Couple B

Her: Ideal if you're a bit tired – and proof you don't have to swing from the chandeliers to have good sex. Plus he can stroke and touch my bottom – men don't think of that enough.

Him: Physically, it's very stimulating, although you don't have to do much work. Good for a Friday night after a long week at work.

Couple C

Her: This makes the pleasure last beyond orgasm as you can fall asleep without your partner having to withdraw. Sometimes, if Mark comes home late, I pretend to be asleep, with my back towards him. He slips into bed and makes love to me, which really turns

Spoons

him on. It turns me on to be 'overpowered' in this way, too.

Him: Everything she says is true.

Is it for, you? Very comfortable for both partners. Penetratlon is deep and can be controlled by the woman. She (or her partner) can also provide extra clitoral stimulation, which is never a bad thing. Great if you're feeling lazy as you don't have to work yourself into a lather for sparks to fly.

Variation: You can turn to face your partner – a tender position but many women find it less exciting.

3. Pole Position

Man lying on his back, the woman sitting on him, facing away

Pleasure Points: 8/10

Couple A

Her: You feel very strong sensations – and because it feels a little naughty, it's even better. You feel daring, almost an exhibitionist. You can also really feel your partner inside you, and get maximum penetration.

Him: I like the slightly voyeuristic side to this, watching your partner moving around and being able to touch her at the same time. Women don't realise how much we love looking at their bottoms – and this is the perfect position for it.

Pole Position

Couple B

Her: You need strong thighs for this one, otherwise you're exhausted long before you're close to orgasm. And if you have a complex about your cellulite, forget it.

Him: I'm not crazy about this as I can't see her face, and I really like watching her expressions during sex.

Couple C

Her: I like it because the woman can take control – and your lover can caress your back and hips.

Him: This made me feel macho. From a sexual point of view it's very exciting – so exciting everything can be over far too quickly.

Is it for you? He can intimately touch your bottom or anus while you can touch his testicles – which can be a turn-on for you both. But it's an acrobatic position, so just pray your legs don't get cramp as you approach the big O.

Variations: Lean backwards or forwards, but gently, as you can painfully yank the penis.

4. Back to Basics (or Doggie Style)

Woman on all fours, man leaning behind her

Pleasure Points: 7/10

Couple A

Her: Very arousing, but it's best after a lot of foreplay.

Back to Basics

Going straight in can be a bit of a shock as penetration is so forceful.

Him: Like all the men I know, I adore this position. The penis is gripped tightly, which is fantastic, and it's so animal, you get completely carried away.

Couple B

Her: You can't take yourself too seriously doing this. If you feel belittled by such a male-dominated position, don't bother, but it's great if you like a no-holds-barred animal romp.

Him: Outstanding – seeing her like this brings out the cave-man in me. But it's so exciting you have to pace yourself, pause from time to time or it'll be over very fast.

Couple C

Her: I'm not a fan of this, it's too crude. But it does feel very intense, especially if he caresses your breasts, back and hips at the same time.

Him: Very sexy, especially if your partner flexes her hips.

Is it for you? Women either love or hate this one because it's so animal. Such deep penetration can be painful, especially if you aren't well lubricated. To get the maximum pleasure, make sure your partner doesn't turn into an over-excited battering ram.

Variations: You can lean up against the wall to shorten the angle of your vagina (handy if you don't want him going so far in), or you can lie flat down on your stomach, or over a pillow, for a more relaxed version.

5. Missionary

The classic position, face to face, him on top of you

Pleasure Points: 6½/10

Couple A

Her: Ideal if communication is important. The pene-tration itself doesn't produce the most pleasurable sensations – but if you put a cushion under the small of your back you can feel your partner more.

Him: Not the most original, but it can be a turn-on to be so in control of your lover and see her lying there below you.

Couple B

Her: Tends to be average, but there is room for improve-ment – just raise your legs. It's also more fun if your partner is in a more upright position.

Him: For me, this is fine. I like the fact that you can kiss each other as you make love.

Couple C

Her: Ideal if you aren't into acrobatics. It doesn't feel that sensational, but you can sometimes gently reach orgasm.

Him: Okay, nothing special, but fine if you aren't looking for unexpected sensations.

Is it for you? You can control the rhythm of your partner and therefore your pleasure. The more you raise your legs, the more your partner can stimulate the front wall

Missionary

of your vagina and your G Spot. It's got a bit of a bad reputation, but this position does have quite a lot going for it – you can stare lovingly into each other's eyes and enjoy the feel of his body covering yours.

Variations: You can raise your legs further and wrap them around his shoulders or bring them back towards your chest. You can also cross your legs around your lover to avoid strain on your inner thighs.

6. The Cat

Woman carried by man, him standing, woman facing him

Pleasure Points: 6/10

Couple A

Her: Great if you love being spontaneous – you can do this in a lift, or against a wall (I kept one leg on the floor). But you need to be really turned on and well lubricated to get decent penetration.

Him: Penetration is deep and it feels wild and rough. Very exciting.

Couple B

Her: There are more comfortable positions, you feel a bit tense because you're worried you're going to fall over. But it feels exciting, all wild and animal.

Him: Okay for a quick one and an explosive orgasm, but you need strong legs and it isn't much good if you want to take your time.

The Cat

Couple C

Her: You have to let yourself go and hope passion takes over. It's quite hard work for your partner, so he starts to breathe heavily, which can be sexy to listen to.

Him: Sexy but not easy. You need to establish a good rhythm to get pleasure, plus you need a firm footing, and strong arms.

Is it for you? The idea of a quick one on the counter definitely has something going for it – problem is, there isn't always a handy counter around. Penetration can be very deep, so if you're not keen on this, make sure he goes easy.

Variations: Unless the man is exceptionally strong, find a wall to lean against, keep one foot on the ground and wrap another around your partner's hips. This can also help keep things going longer. Or edge your bottom on a counter for support.

7. The Wheelbarrow

Man on his knees, supporting woman (who is on her back) by the hips

Pleasure Points: 6/10

Couple A

Her: Like the missionary position, but less comfortable. You're completely manipulated by the man. When he knows what he's doing, it's good. And the fact that your body is arched up, offered to him, can be exciting.

The Wheelbarrow

Him: You're having to support her, so you don't have any hands free to touch her, which can be a drag. It's particularly annoying as she looks very tempting, arched up like that.

Couple B

Her: Average. You feel too spread out and you can't do a thing.

Him: More fun for the man. You feel quite selfish.

Couple C

Her: Quite hard work, but my partner seemed to enjoy it.

Him: She's arched up towards you, so you're gripped nice and tightly, but it takes so much effort to support her it becomes rather tricky.

Is it for you? This guarantees intense penetration – and as your body's stretched so tightly your vaginal muscles are tightly gripping his penis. This can give very intense contractions. However, watch out if your partner has dodgy knees or you have a bad back. However, it's great if you have small breasts and feel self-conscious about them – leaning back makes them look gorgeous.

Variation: Try lying out over the edge of the bed with him kneeling on the floor. This gives a similar effect, but he doesn't have to support you.

8. Dizzy Heights

Man standing behind woman, her back to him, leaning over

Pleasure Points: 6/10

Couple A

Her: Strong contact and can be great if you fantasise about the thought of anal sex, but don't want to go through with the reality.

Him: Exciting, but only as part of the lovemaking. I'd prefer not to climax in this position as I can't see much of her body and none of her face – so I feel as if I'm on my own, masturbating.

Couple B

Her: It makes you feel rather passive. The main worry is keeping your balance, which can be difficult unless your partner has a strong grip on you. You need to be completely in tune with him and very turned on to deal with this 'Darling, take me' type of position.

Him: Really exciting, and you can change rhythm, but it can be lonely to go the whole way like this.

Couple C

Her: If you like torrid sex for its own sake, go for it! Your partner needs to take care not to be too brutal as penetration is deep, which can be painful.

Him: From a sexual point of view, it's pure and powerful, but lacks tenderness and communication.

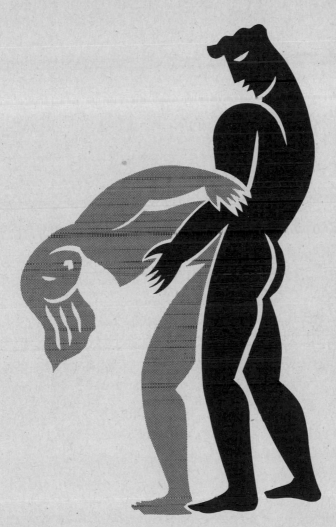

Dizzy Heights

Is it for you? Losing your balance is the number one danger in this position, so it can be handy to find a wall or table to lean against. And remember, to even get to base one, you need to be slightly on your toes, or your lover will have to support himself on slightly bent knees.

Variations: Don't try any — it's tricky enough as it is — but you can try standing on a step, so you don't have to balance on your toes.

9. The Phoenix

Woman on her back, legs raised, facing man, who holds her by the ankles

Pleasure Points: 9/10–2/10

Couple A

Her: Zero, you feel powerless. The main advantage is very deep penetration, which can be fun.

Him: I know Justine didn't like this, I can see why. But from my point of view, what a feeling of power! Plus you penetrate very deeply and are gripped very tightly. Very exciting!

Couple B

Her: I felt like a sex object; you're controlled by your partner and can't do anything. I felt very uncomfortable.

Him: This is very exciting if you like to dominate — it's like having your own personal slave-girl in a harem.

The Phoenix

Couple C

Her: I quite enjoyed this – I have a bit of a fantasy about being dominated, so mentally I found it a turn-on. Physically though I couldn't move at all; perhaps it's more fun in theory than practice.

Him: Maximum penetration and a great view and a feeling of power – great fun, but I did feel a bit selfish.

Is it for you? If you aren't supple, you'll find this difficult. It can be a turn-on to play slave-girl for the night, but it can be frustrating not being able to move your hips at all.

Variation: Put a pillow under your bottom, rest on your forearms and put your ankles on his shoulders. You'll be able to move a bit more freely and he can grasp your bottom to support you a little more.

10. Sideways Seduction

Both partners facing each other on their sides, legs entwined

Pleasure Points: 5/10

Couple A

Her: Comfortable, intimate and very exciting. It's good if you move your legs to vary the angle of penetration.

Him: Not bad for lazy evenings. You can also kiss and talk to one another if you like.

Sideways Seduction

Couple B

Her: This is almost funny. You're not that stable on your side, so it can help to lean back against a pillow, but it's a gentle, close way to lead up to a climax.

Him: The main advantage is that you can touch your partner all over, but you quickly find yourself wanting to move on to more powerful things.

Couple C

Her: I felt a pain in my lower abdomen I'd never felt before – anyway I didn't feel very relaxed or comfortable.

Him: I'm sorry Roz felt pain because I liked this. I felt really close to her and because it's not that exciting physically, you can touch all of her and kiss her face.

Is it for you? The more supple the man is in his back the more he'll be able to stimulate you, but you probably won't wake the neighbours in this position.

Variations: Some extra gymnastics can help. Move your legs on top of his and raise them vertically, or fold them back towards your chest.

➡ Yes, you *can* have a vaginal orgasm

Before we go any further – it's a fact that most women do not have orgasm through the action of the penis in the vagina. Many studies show that less than a quarter of women often climax this way – mostly it takes oral sex or masturbation during sex to do the trick. Yet many of us are still convinced we 'should' be able to come this way – that's partly why we feel tempted to fake orgasm sometimes. We feel that a 'real' woman would have an orgasm through a penis in her vagina, and we don't want to be seen as less than a real woman!

So, if you do not orgasm via penetrative sex, and are happy climaxing through oral sex or by giving yourself a helping hand, that's fine. A vaginal orgasm is not superior to any other – it's just another path to pleasure you might like to explore some day.

Research has shown that one of the main problems with penis-in-vagina sex – what the sex therapists call 'penetrative sex' – is that 80 per cent of the time the man enters the woman before she is ready. Contrary to popular misconception, being wet does not mean you're ready – it's just one of the most obvious signs. Another misconception is that the vagina is ready for orgasm once the entrance has swelled and opened up slightly. Again, it's a sign you're on your way, but nowhere near a climax. In fact, when you are really ready to orgasm, the vaginal opening actually decreases in size, allowing it to grip the penis. This is because at the point of orgasm your vagina lengthens and balloons internally. This 'tenting' effect means a penis could slip out if it wasn't gripped somewhere.

However, let's assume your foreplay has been fantastic, you're both in the mood – and you fancy the idea of trying for a vaginal orgasm. Now what?

- Wait until you reach the point where you're both very excited – the point where he would normally enter you. But don't let him – at least not yet.

- Ask him to take his penis in his hand and gently rub your clitoris with it. The idea is to tease you and let you know he could enter you . . . but he's going to wait. The longer he can hold off (even if you're beside yourself with desire) the better the result will be.

- Let him enter you very slowly, just the tip. Then slowly withdraw again. Repeat this teasing in and out game, gradually inserting more and more of his penis.

- Make sure he doesn't insert all of his penis – what you're trying to do is gently tease your clitoris, not bang against it. This might sound like torture but the good news is that while you're teasing each other, you're both building your excitement. And the longer you wait the more exciting it will be – for both of you.

- If your partner is unwilling to try this technique, you can still subtly control his speed and movements. This is not as satisfactory as having a willing partner, but if you show him the ropes a few times (and you both have a massive climax) it may be just the encouragement he needs.

- If he comes in too fast or too strongly, use your thighs to control him. In the missionary position, for example, if you tend to lie with your legs apart, try wrapping them around his waist, so he can't thrust as hard or fast.

- As he moves his penis into you, squeeze your thighs together; this will slow his movements and stop him pushing so hard into you. By squeezing with your thighs you can also control how much of his penis he can thrust into you – he will only be able to go in as far as you let him. Then you can try the slow and teasing technique for yourself.

↦ Seven steps to joygasmic sex

There's one glorious truth about the female orgasm – when you've experienced it once, you'll want to experience it again. Although there may be one method which nearly always works for you, experimenting may show you other routes to pleasure. The idea is to learn by doing . . . so enjoy!

Step 1: Body bliss

It's hard to feel sexy if you don't like the way you look. If you think you're too fat (women often do, even when they're not) you may not want to try new sexual positions, worried that you'll look 'ugly' or ungainly. Sex experts call this process 'armouring', when we start to feel so negative about our body image that anxiety gets mixed in with our pleasure. We can become so tense that we don't get wet or get caught up in the pleasure enough to climax. The only way out is to reverse your attitude. Get undressed. Stand in front of a mirror and, running your hands over your body, repeat: 'I am beautiful.' Do it every day until it sinks in. Yes, you'll feel silly but you're not likely to feel comfortable letting your partner see you naked if you're not comfortable looking at yourself. It may encourage you to know that many prostitutes say they are often paid simply to take their clothes off and walk around. They know men are turned on by the sight of a naked woman, whatever her shape.

Step 2: Suit yourself

Virtually all women who masturbate can bring them-selves to a climax – and what you learn on your own you can teach to your partner. Masturbation shows you which parts of your body are most easily aroused, what kind of touch helps you come and what touch gives you the most satisfying orgasm. It helps you to find your own particular pleasure pattern. Sara explains, 'I am a strong independent woman, so I love it when a man takes control in bed. But if a partner hasn't found my right spot, I'm not ashamed to show him – after all, it is my moment.'

Step 3: Umm, just there . . .

As Marie said earlier, men have a tendency to treat a clitoris like a lift button – they think the more they press it, the quicker you'll zoom to the top. This isn't because your partner doesn't care, it's more because the penis is less sensitive than the clitoris. He might have found a firm touch works wonders with him – and naturally assumes it will do the same for you.

Unfortunately, he's wrong. The best movements to turn on women are ones working around the base of the clitoris, rather than touching it directly. And, unlike a penis, a lighter touch is almost more effective than firm pressure. The trick is how to get this news across to your partner without turning your lovemaking into a driving lesson: Turn right! Left! Emergency stop!

Sex experts say talking to your lover is possibly the best thing you can do for your sex life. Look at it this way – his ego is on your side. He wants to be a good lover and to please you, so gently suggesting that he touches you 'like this . . . ' can work wonders. For example, Tracey says, 'Until recently I'd only experienced orgasm once, through oral sex. I forgot about it and accepted penetrative sex for what it was. Then I started having a sexual relationship with a good friend of mine. After a while we told each other what turned us on. It's made so much difference to the sex.'

Step 4: Wet, wet, wet

Lubrication is crucial to your orgasm, but your levels can vary depending on what time of the month it is, how much you smoke and drink, and how tense you are. So, if you are feeling dry, don't stuff him in anyway, figuring things will moisten up when you get going. They won't; instead you're more likely to create a vicious circle of mental warfare where the sex becomes so painful you tense up and become even more dry.

The easiest solution is adding saliva to the mix; otherwise try a water-based lubricant, available without a prescription from the chemist.

Step 5: Mind power

When we think of erogenous zones we usually focus between the legs, but in fact your brain is your body's sexiest organ, which means ecstasy depends on letting go mentally. That's why the harder you strain for an orgasm the more elusive it becomes. Rachel explains, 'Sometimes I don't climax, usually because I'm tired or because I'm only having sex because my partner wants me to. Occasionally I get too anxious that I will not climax and then it rarely seems to happen.' Adds Helen, 'If you start thinking, "Oh no, I'm not going to come," or you start to worry too much, you don't come. I once had a boyfriend who would ask every five minutes if I was going to come – which put me off track totally.'

The good news is that we can train our minds to improve sex. You can turn yourself on in advance by imagining what you want to happen when you're with your lover, so that when you do meet in the flesh you're raring to go.

Rebecca tried this method one weekend when she knew she was going to see her boyfriend: 'I thought about the look he gave me when he wanted to have sex and the things he could do to me. By the time we got together I was ready to tear off his clothes. It blew us both away.'

Step 6: Oral meltdown

There's nothing like oral sex to bring a woman to orgasm – basically most women say it's a sure-fire method for them. If he's less than experienced you can position yourself by rotating your pelvis as he licks. It also helps if you let him know you're having a good time; anything from moans and sighs to threats of murder if he stops should encourage him in his efforts. You may even discover a whole new range of pleasures to share. Tracey says, 'I told my current partner I could only orgasm through oral sex, but we found out that after I have been stimulated that way, if

I have sex in a certain position against a wall, my G Spot can be found and I can also have an orgasm through penetrative sex.'

Step 7: Often is best

Orgasm has this in common with most physical exercise – the more you do it, the easier it gets. At first, having an orgasm can be scary, as you reveal the deepest, most vulnerable side of yourself. Explains Leane, 'I have had an orgasm, but it is difficult. My body becomes tense when I feel myself starting to let go and my arms straighten very quickly, pushing my boyfriend away. It's because I hate the feeling of "letting myself go", yet a deep curiosity makes me want to continue. For me, sex is brilliant in theory, but not always in practice.'

Della adds this insight: 'Sometimes I don't come. I get very tense, yet remain switched-on for hours afterwards. The more dramatic the lovemaking, the more intense the frustration . . . I think my problem may be to do with my childhood, when I was taught that sex was dirty and shameful, something to be hidden.'

If orgasm is elusive for you because you also hate the feeling of letting go, it's worth remembering that relationship experts say sexual self-confidence – and more orgasms – can be achieved through facing your fears and finding they're not so bad after all. There's nothing so exciting as sharing the deepest parts of your personality – and finding that you are still loved. What could be more liberating?

↔ The total-body orgasm

It's one of the ironies of life: sometimes we can get so focused on having an orgasm that we find it difficult to enjoy the rest of our lovemaking – and if we can't enjoy lovemaking there's no way we're going to climax.

That's why sex therapists often encourage women to relax and enjoy the ride, instead of focusing on the destination. Here are just a few of the techniques they use:

Like your body. Study your naked body carefully in a mirror. Make a mental list of all the nice bits. It's a fact that most men do not judge us as harshly as we judge ourselves – they tend to gloss over the zones you hate and happily zoom in on the bits they find lovely.

Unfortunately, because we don't see many naked bodies (except the perfect ones flaunted by models and film stars), we often get a distorted view of what real women's bodies look like. Sex therapists often show their clients pictures of naked people to help them realise we come in a variety of different shapes and sizes. So, the next time you're at the gym or are trying on clothes in a communal changing room, take a look around. The women your man has previously experienced are unlikely to look like cellulite-free models and are more likely to look like you.

Realise human scents are normal. We've been trained to think of normal female smells as offensive. Provided you shower or bath every day and don't have any infections, you'll smell like all other healthy young women – a scent men find pleasurable and exciting.

Accept that being selfish in bed is okay. Love-making isn't just about giving pleasure and worrying if you're turning him on. Make sure you get your share too – let him turn you on.

Stop 'spectatoring'. One of the most important steps in getting maximum pleasure in bed is to learn how to focus on the sensations and not allow other thoughts to distract you. If you find yourself starting to wonder if you're boring him, or he's turned off by your thighs, you are doing what sex therapists call 'spectatoring'. In other words, you don't feel totally enthralled by your lovemaking – instead it's as if you're a spectator watching someone else go through the motions of making love.

Of course, it's easier said than done to stop doing this, but it does come with practice. At first you'll have to work hard to fight off intrusive thoughts, but try focusing on the physical sensations – how does his hand feel on your body, what does he smell like? Concentrate on the sound of your breathing, the feel of his skin against yours. It can also help to look deep into his eyes. To help even more, therapists often recommend what they call 'sensate focusing' exercises – which help you focus on the sensations your body is feeling.

Sensate focusing exercises

The aim of these exercises is to take the focus off intercourse and discover how different sensations really feel. So, during each phase you must agree not to have sexual intercourse – even when the task is finished.

- Your partner caresses you while you lie perfectly still. However, he must avoid touching your genitals or breasts – and you don't have sex. Make sure you use all your five senses: touch, taste, smell, sight and sound. You can play music or revel in silence and the sound of your own breathing – whatever you want. Tell him what you like, suggesting how he could make it better; for example, 'When you kiss my ear lobe like that it's nice, but it could be even better if you blew gently over it.' After a while, swap places. It's important you repeat this exercise a few times to discover the wide range of sensations that turn you on. You could even decide that all you'll do for a fortnight or a month are these exercises – that way the pressure is really off you both.

- After several sessions like this, the next phase is to move on to touching your breasts and genitals. Again, as your partner caresses you with his hands, body or mouth, tell him what you like by talking, nodding, smiling, murmuring or moving his hand. The aim of this exercise is not to reach orgasm, but to learn how sensations can be enjoyed for the pleasure in themselves. So again, try and avoid intercourse. If your partner gets too excited, ease back until he's cooled down, then continue.

- The next step is penetration. After your sensate focusing foreplay, when you are both excited and ready, he can penetrate you. Once this has been achieved, both partners should lie still, just enjoying the sensation of being so close, poised on the brink of exquisite pleasure. If the man starts to lose his erection he can move slightly to maintain it. Try contracting your vaginal muscles (the same ones you use to stop the flow of urine). Stay like this for several minutes, but withdraw before either of you has an orgasm. Repeat this exercise for several nights – but always stop short of orgasm.

- Now take it in turns to move. You move first, concentrating on your own sensations. Later he takes his turn. Make sure you both use only slow, gentle movements so you can focus on how your body feels. Every so often, withdraw and keep pleasuring each other. After several sessions, if you both agree, you can continue your lovemaking to the point of orgasm.

The touch exercise

This is a playful variation on the sensate focus exercises. Take it in turns to try it on different parts of your bodies – and remember to let each other know what feels good. It's important to remember that everyone is turned on by different things. No matter how experienced the guy is, you are unique and it's up to you to show him what turns you on. If he asks, you don't have to put it into words; simply move his hands or mouth to where it feels best.

With the hands try:

- Stroking
- Feather-light trailing fingers
- Rubbing
- Pinching
- Scratching gently

- Scratching hard
- Massaging
- Massaging with knuckles
- Tickling
- Smacking
- Pummelling

With the mouth try:

- Kissing with mouth closed
- Kissing with mouth open
- Licking with a soft tongue
- Licking with a rigid tongue
- Sucking gently
- Sucking hard
- Blowing
- Nibbling
- Biting

Chapter 8

SAME BOY, NEW JOY

↔ How to give your relationship a sexual makeover

↔ Bed, bed, stockroom, bed

↔ Kinky sex – and the last taboo

↔ Toning your sexual muscles

'Sex has to be physical but not rushed, starting with a massage with oils, followed by plenty of foreplay, otherwise I'll never even get close to an orgasm.'

Sara

'If my partner feels like selfishly having a "quickie" and isn't interested in foreplay or helping me climax I get very frustrated and want to kick him out of bed. Sex is made good by two people taking part, it's not just for the man's pleasure.'

Suzie

►► How to give your relationship a sexual makeover

When you first get together with a new partner the sex is nearly always exciting – merely because it's new. You're both so keen to get your hands on each other, just a glance across the room can get you going.

However, within a few years, or months, the heavy breathing can turn to sighs of boredom as you contemplate sex in the same position, in the same bed with the same man. Sure, it's cosy and intimate – but probably not all that exciting, is it?

The good news is that sex therapists say there are relatively easy ways to put fire back into your sex life – the less-good news is that you have to make a concentrated effort to make love in a different way. This may seem silly and mechanical at first (after all, we often imagine that good sex is just 'spontaneous' – a matter of pure chemistry), but the fact is, all this thinking about sex and planning for it is exactly what you did in the early days of your relationship. That is the one key reason the sex was so good.

So here, if you're in the mood to try a little something new, is a five-step makeover to stoke up your sexual fires.

Step 1: The celibacy vow

Strange but true – the quickest way to heat up your sex life is to stop making love for a while. This works on the principle that if you give anyone unlimited access to anything, eventually it becomes ho-hum.

The power of sexual denial is equally strong – with emphasis on the *denial*. There's a big difference between unconsciously skipping sex because you can't be bothered and saying, 'Not tonight. I want you, but I want to savour this feeling.' (This is best said with a smile, so no one feels punished.)

Says Bella, 'In the early days Paul and I made love nearly every day, but somewhere along the line it stopped. Then he had to go to Scotland for six months for work. When we were away from each other, every weekend meeting was charged with sexual tension. It was so exciting!' Now, although Paul is back home with Bella again, they deliberately don't make love for several days in a row: 'We wait until we can't take it any more, then make passionate love wherever the mood strikes.'

Step 2: Become a tease

If you're in a settled relationship, think about this: when was the last time you made love with some of your clothes still on? Probably back at the start, right? Too many of us think nudity equals naturalness so, once we become regular lovers, we remove our clothes with as little pomp and ceremony as possible. The advice from the sex therapists is simple: slow down.

Starting sex with some of your clothes still on gives you more time for long kisses and foreplay, plus it allows more chance for you both to indulge in seductive games: keeping on your hold-up stockings, staging a for-his-eyes-only strip in a push-up bra and French knickers. Yes, it's a bit of a cliché, but if he enjoys the sight of you in lacy lingerie, why argue?

If the thought of prancing around in your underwear in the living room makes you cringe, skip this one – it won't be an erotic treat for him if you're looking embarrassed. If you fancy the idea, but feel a little shy, it may help to know about a recent relationship survey. Of the 1,000 men who were asked for their favourite turn-ons, 92 per cent said they were turned on by lingerie and 73 per cent said they used stimulation such as this to keep up the heat in their relationships.

Step 3: Enjoy the build-up

This may sound a strange thing to say in a book about your orgasm, but if you want really good sex it pays to forget about your destination and concentrate on the pleasures of the journey. Which brings us again to the 'sensate focusing exercises' we learnt in Chapter 7. These basic lovemaking techniques are widely taught by sex therapists as they help you to focus on feeling good all over.

Remember, sensate focusing techniques are about playing with each other's bodies, rather than heading straight for intercourse. Set aside at least half an hour, get naked and take turns caressing each other (making sure to stay well clear of the usual erogenous zones). Whoever's on the receiving end should concentrate on their own sensations. Above all, take it slowly – stroke and tease each other for as long as you can stand it before you move on to the more familiar hot spots. The odds are, once you do get down to raw sex, you'll both be teetering on the edge of a fantastic orgasm.

Step 4: It's playtime

Sex toys are just like any other fashion accessory: a little extra to liven things up. What you use is up to you – many of the best toys are lying around your home right now: perfumed candles can be used to delight your senses, ice cubes will give your bare skin a frisson of pleasure, whipped cream adds a sweetness to oral sex, silk scarves can double as sexy blindfolds or handcuffs . . . the possibilities are as endless as your imagination.

'I like to play at the weekends. Last week we had a candlelit bath with perfumed oils. For a couple of weeks before that we took turns reading sexual fantasies aloud from a book I'd bought. Sometimes we'd even try to act them out.'

Melanie

On the more technical side, although vibrators are still something of a taboo (many of us imagine they're 'dirty' or only used by sad women who can't get a real man), sales are soaring. What's more, mail-order agencies report that many customers are young women who are using a vibrator as part of their sex life, rather than just a substitute for one.

'Using a vibrator guarantees an orgasm for me – I get through a lot of batteries! I also get very turned on watching sexy films or reading porn magazines – but I only do this about once every six months. If I did it more I feel it would lose its effect.'

Rachel

Rachel is not alone in enjoying spicy videos. It's been estimated that women account for perhaps 40 per cent of the estimated 100 million rentals of X-rated videos in Britain each year.

Step 5: Go for it!

Finally, it's time to connect, but instead of him just climbing on top for ten minutes, try turning it into a *Kama-sutra* experience. First, get him to lie on his back while you slowly straddle him. Don't rush things; just touch each other and lie there, enjoying the closeness of body contact. Relish the sensations of the touch and scent of your bodies.

After a few minutes, slowly guide the tip of his penis inside you. Again, stop and savour the experience. Start at a slow pace, building up and up. Then, just before you peak, stop for a few minutes, then start the whole thing over again. Repeat until you simply can't stop.

To add even more spice to your lovemaking, you can try doing all this while you're both lightly blind-folded. This can make you more acutely aware of the sensations your body is feeling.

➮ Sex in weird places

Why are we so attracted to the idea of sex somewhere out of the ordinary?

Beds are perfect for sex ... they're flat, soft, comfortable. So why is it that the most exciting sex often happens anyplace but in bed?

The answer may be that sex away from the sheets is, quite simply, more memorable. If you plotted the average sexual graph it would go something like this: bed, bed, bed, office stockroom, bed, bed, bed, bed. On that basis, which occasion would you be most likely to remember?

Coupled with the memorability of the event is the idea that sex in strange places is somehow more lustful and wild. You can tell yourself that lust has taken you over – you just can't stop yourself. Anna explains the appeal for her: 'Sometimes it's the situation rather than the actual act. After all, sex is just sex, but my imagination plays a big part. For example, I revel in the risk of being discovered. Twice I've had sex in my living room while my flatmates were asleep upstairs. The thought of being caught only added to my excitement and made my climax quicker and more intense.'

So, if you enjoy sex in unusual places, does it mean you have no respect for authority? Probably not. Psychologists say people who relish the chance of being caught *in flagrante delicto* often have a real respect for society and its rules. After all, there's no excitement in breaking a rule you haven't noticed in the first place.

'I get a kick out of the secrecy of it, and the naughtiness. There are about half a dozen places in my workplace where I've had sex. It's a turn-on to know something that nobody else knows. Every time I pass this desk or the stairs to the roof I think, "That's where I had Philip." It's a private joke between me and myself.'

Ruth

Above all, we have sex in unusual places because we want our lover to see us as special and unique (and we want to see ourselves that way too). We want to prove we're not stuck in a passionless rut – that we're exciting, dangerous and wild, as well as reliable and loving.

We don't need to choose somewhere very unusual for this effect to work either – it can be just as exciting to let rip on the privacy of your kitchen floor as in the middle of a public park. 'Girl makes out with partner on bathroom tiles in privacy of own home' is hardly the stuff of headlines, but you can be sure it feels like world news at the time!

➤ How kinky is too kinky?

He wants to try something new in bed . . . something *very* new. Where do you draw the line?

Let's say one night your much-adored lover produces a cucumber not intended for the evening salad. Or perhaps he shocks you by 'talking dirty' while making love. Or whips out some scarves and suggests tying you up. Whatever it is, let's say that the prospect appeals to you as much as eating live lizards – but the last thing you want to be is a prude, right? And relationships are all about compromise, right? So where's the harm, right?

Wrong. Don't be too quick to go along with a sexual suggestion which makes you uneasy, however insistent your partner is that it's 'only a bit of fun'. Trust your instincts. If you're not comfortable with the suggestion, you need to explore why you don't want to do something and why he does.

The truth is, a kinky suggestion can force into the open aspects of your relationship you might prefer to ignore. People often reveal their most intimate, uninhibited selves through sex, and if you don't like what you've learnt about him your relationship can be threatened – not to mention your ability to have orgasms with him.

It's disturbing when somebody you thought you knew inside out reveals a side you find hard to accept. Even talking about kinky sex in the abstract makes people nervous. On one level we all make jokes about sex that's a little out of the ordinary. We giggle with our girlfriends over saucy stories in the newspapers about men who want to wear rubber (or want their girlfriends to wear it) – but it's not quite so funny if the person snapping on the rubber gloves is the boyfriend you thought you knew so well.

Kinky sex can also force you to think about your own desires. Say you think of yourself as 'a nice girl', yet he persuades you to try sex wearing nothing but your high heels and – and you love it. Does that mean you're not 'nice' anymore?

If you're both happy

The truth about kinky sex is pretty simple: if you both genuinely enjoy dressing up, talking dirty or spanking, then it can be 'just a bit of fun'. You can take it as far as you like, or try out a fantasy that would be dangerous or disgusting in real life.

'I'd hate to be a hooker in reality, but when I pretend with my boyfriend it's a sleazy turn-on. I pretend I'm a woman who's sex mad and experienced.'

Kim

Exploring your sexual quirks like this can genuinely bring the two of you closer together. Plus, one person's kinky sex is another person's ho-hum lovemaking. So, before you throw your hands up in horror at a suggestion, ask yourself if you're genuinely shocked – or if you just feel that as 'a nice girl' you *ought* to be shocked.

'I remember once suggesting to a boyfriend that I go on top. He just stared at me and said, "You're weird." The relationship, not surprisingly, ended soon after that.'

Lucy

What's naughty – and what's perverse?

Sometimes it can be surprisingly difficult to work out the difference between a suggestion that's merely adventurous – and one which is perverse. This is because part of you might find it a turn-on, yet another part of you feels unhappy. You may also feel merely curious, thinking, 'Perhaps I might like it if I tried it?'

Relationship therapists have this advice: what makes something perverse or not is whether it furthers the relationship or attacks it. Does it, in the long run, bring you closer? Is there a basic attitude of concern and compassion between you, or do you feel controlled and betrayed?

For example, your boyfriend may try to persuade you that a threesome with your girlfriend is just a laugh, yet you sense that what really turns him on is having total control over your life, even if you hate it. Understandably, you resent being belittled. Also, think how his suggestion was made; was it a demand ('You will do this or else') or was it presented more along the lines of: 'This is how I feel . . . are you interested?' It's a lot easier to try a saucy suggestion when it's not forced upon you. How does his suggestion fit in with how he treats you generally?

'Normally I quite enjoy talking dirty, but only if I feel the man respects me. I think you'll know from a man's behaviour outside bed whether he's using the words just to pep up sex or whether he really thinks you are a slut. Towards the end of my last relationship I got very uncomfortable when he talked dirty during sex because he'd started treating me badly in the relationship. His angry words during sex reflected his general anger towards me.'

Stacy

Not again?

A common fear about going along with a kinky suggestion that doesn't thrill you, but doesn't repulse you either, is that you'll be expected to do it all the time. Let's say you let him video your lovemaking once and found you didn't like it – but what if he had a great time and wants to install the camera in your bedroom?

Ask yourself why he loves doing something with someone who's not enjoying it at all? If he's pushing you around like this, it's not going to be good sex for you (or a good relationship, come to that).

However, what if you feel he's definitely still loving, and he isn't forcing you . . . but you still really don't like the idea he's suggesting? In this case, be tactful when you turn him down, otherwise you risk ruining the atmosphere of give and take that's so vital for good sex. If you don't at least hear out his reasons for asking you to dress up like Fifi, the French maid, you set yourself up for a curt refusal next time you have a suggestion of your own, like, 'How about a bit more foreplay before you enter me?'

Asking yourself a few questions may help you decide how far you wish to go in bed. We all have our own limits and you don't have to justify yours to him – or anyone else.

➼ The last taboo

Perhaps the most startling 'kinky' idea is anal sex. Sex researchers say it's incredibly difficult to find information on this subject. The Sexual Behaviour In Britain survey (based on the responses of 20,000 people) found 12.9 per cent of women reported trying anal sex at least once, compared to 13.9 per cent of men. More women in their late teens and twenties reported trying it than any other age group. Yet, other major international surveys have found different figures: 20 per cent, 40 per cent and even up to 72 per cent of all women trying anal sex at least once. To be honest, the figures vary so wildly the only thing they show is that it's hard to get an honest answer out of anyone, including the one we most want to hear: what's in it for women?

'It's a combination of things for me. I feel really sexy and without limits. And I admit I like the idea that it's naughty and dirty. It's like my guilty secret.'

Kerry

'I'm quite bossy in daily life – so I think it gives men the chance to dominate me in bed, which I enjoy. It gives me a thrill that men get off on it. They enjoy the power, I think.'

Karin

Trust also plays a part. For many women anal sex is something they save for one special man they trust completely.

'I know my boyfriend would stop as soon as I told him. And I set the pace. He holds still and I move against him. You have to really trust your lover a lot because if he was just out for himself, he could really hurt you.'

Maria

Although some women enjoy anal sex, it's fair to say it is more popular with men. Partly, this is because the back passage can provide greater friction around the penis, but more than that, there are visual turn-ons (he can see your rear) plus it makes men feel very powerful and in control. Add the element of raw, animal passion and the hint of taboo, even seedy, pleasure and you've got a combination which proves irresistible for many men.

To some extent, the sexes' different interest in anal sex is also to do with our different anatomies. About two inches up a man's rectum is a very sensitive spot, near the prostate gland. (This gland produces seminal fluid.) Many men find having this area massaged with a finger is very exciting and it can even trigger orgasms. This does not mean they are homosexual; all men have the capacity to be stimulated in this way. It's just a quirk of the male anatomy. Plus, the area between the base of the penis and the anus – the perineum – is very sensitive in men. With so much potential for pleasure in their own rear ends, it's no wonder many men assume women will enjoy anal sex.

No thanks

What men can forget is that the potential for physical pain is only too real for women, which means even the thought of anal sex can send our sex drives plummeting. Physical complications are rare, but may include soreness and bleeding in the anal area. More extreme complications can include infections and, very rarely, incontinence.

'I don't fancy the idea of anal sex. I don't have sexual hang-ups, but it's important to say "No" to things you don't like. When my boyfriend brings up the idea I say, "Okay, if you let me do it to you first, with my fingers." That stops him in his tracks. He says it would hurt. So I say, "Why would it be different for me?"'

Rosie

'My boyfriend nagged me for months to try it. I gave in because I felt he'd think I was a prude if I didn't. But it hurt and I started crying. Then we had a huge argument.'

Lynn

A woman can also feel turned off by anal sex because she wonders if it means he thinks of her as a slut, or nothing more than a sex toy. Or could it mean that he's secretly gay? Sex therapists say a man who enjoys

anal sex is not necessarily gay or bisexual; many hetero-
sexual men are just as keen.

One final word: anal sex is a very high-risk activity
for the transmission of sexually transmitted diseases,
including the HIV virus. The inner walls of the rectum
aren't as strong or flexible as those in the vagina.
Thinner, more delicate walls mean you can suffer tiny
cuts and bruises more easily and HIV-infected blood
or semen can pass into your bloodstream. Condoms and
water-based lubricants (oil-based ones can rot latex)
aren't a luxury here, they're a life-saving necessity.

⇥ The orgasm workout

It seems everything can be improved by exercise – and
your climax is no exception – but you need to know the
right muscles to exercise.

Women can train their internal muscles to become
more toned and gripping; this not only thrills your lover,
but it can also give you bigger, better orgasms, and
more of them. Here's how . . .

The muscle in question is the pubococcygeus (PC)
or pelvic-floor muscle. As a rough guide, it's the muscle you clench when you're at an outdoor concert and
you can't stand the idea of going to the loo. When you
orgasm, the wave-like clenching you feel is your PC
muscle rhythmically contracting. About an inch wide,
it runs in a flexible figure-of-eight shape from your
tail-bone at the back to your vagina in the front, link-
ing the crucial bits in between, including your rectum
or back passage, your bladder and your urethra (the
outlet from your bladder). Basically, it's like the floor of

your body, holding everything in place – hence its name.

Unlike the vaginal walls, which are pretty nerveless, the PC muscle (which surrounds the middle of the vagina) is rich in nerve endings. This means that the fitter the muscle, the more blood reaches those nerves, and the more sensation you feel, hence the easier (and more intense) your orgasms become. As a happy side effect, if you're internally toned you can also bring your lover to a screaming frenzy merely by flexing yourself inside.

Toning internally

You need to do what are known as Kegel exercises, after their inventor in the 1950s, Dr Kegel. Start by identifying your PC muscle by clenching inwardly, as if you're trying to stop going to the toilet midway. Now pulse (contract and release) twenty times, as fast as you can. Doctors recommend that you do this up to twenty times a day. In four weeks you'll notice a real difference.

For a more structured approach try the following exercises for thirty minutes a day and you will feel the difference in weeks, reaching Olympic-level toning in six months:

PC pulse. Contract and release your PC muscle in fast pulses for about five minutes. At first you may find this tricky, as the muscles around your stomach will probably tense as well. However, when you have pinpointed the PC, practise tensing it in time with your breathing; breathe in while you contract, breathe out while you relax. You may feel some tingling. This shows the exercise is working as the blood is flowing faster through the muscle.

PC clench. When you can isolate your PC, move on to the more concentrated clench. Breathe in, contract the muscle and hold in for six seconds, as if you are trying to hold a full bladder. When you breathe out, bear down slightly. Continue the sequence for five minutes.

Pelvic roll. Lie on the floor with your knees up, or kneel with a pillow between your legs. With your stomach loose, breathe in, push your pelvis into the floor. As you breathe out, rotate your pelvis forward. Do this rocking exercise for five minutes.

These exercises can benefit any woman, but they are especially recommended for women who have given birth, and notice a loss of vaginal tightness and sensation.

Chapter 9

CALLING ALL BEDROOM ACTRESSES

➤➤ Why women fake orgasm – or don't

➤➤ The biggest sin – or no big deal?

➤➤ Why embarrassing noises and elbows in the ribs are part of the fun

➤➤ Distractions – and how to rekindle the fire

'I've never faked and I never will. I know I sound too good to be true, but if I get bored or tired I ask them to stop. Plus I think a man can tell if you've faked.'

Scarlet

'I have faked. Sometimes because I didn't want to hurt my partner's feelings, other times so that it would end sooner. I try not to do it anymore, although I still find it hard to tell a man what I like or where to touch me. I want to, but I feel silly.'

Jo

➼ Real women confess

Why I fake orgasm . . .

'My first orgasm with my ex-boyfriend was very dramatic – my body shook and I cried – but then he expected the earth to move every time. Afterwards he'd ask, "Did anything happen?" and if I hadn't come he'd feel rejected. This meant I avoided sex so that I didn't have to listen to his questioning, or I'd fake, roll over and go to sleep.'

Leane

'I've made the usual noises and panted as if I've been taken to the enchanted forest. I've even looked my partner in the eye and said, "Thank you". I'm not sure if I convinced the guy but I couldn't face the conversation about, "Why do you think you didn't come?" Although my sexual confidence has grown a lot in the past few years, at times like that I see myself as a 24-year-old with the maturity of an 18-year-old, the sexual needs of a convent of nuns and the emotional skills of a gnat.'

Anna

'I often fake during intercourse, mainly because of my lover's feelings and also so that he doesn't think there is something wrong with me. I know there isn't because I know my own body very well, but I have to be completely still to concentrate on my orgasm. So, if my partner keeps still inside me as I masturbate, I'm fine. But that isn't very easy as his instinct is to thrust in and out.'

Joanna

'I faked, until I got found out. My partner and I spend hours making love, but sometimes he wants to go on too long. So in the past, just to get it over with, I'd fake. But one night my lover said, "Please don't fake with me." I was so shocked! Now I don't bother faking. I just say it's not going to happen and we're fine about it. There's always the next time.'

Sharon

. . . and why I don't

'I feel I don't have to fake; because I am friends with my sexual partner we are able to talk about things openly. I'll definitely tell any sexual partner I may have in the future, what I like. I've learnt it's an advantage to my enjoyment.'

Tracey

'I don't fake. It's important to be able to trust each other in a relationship. If I don't feel like having sex any more I just tell my partner – but I try to get across that it's not his fault. I give him a big hug and tell him I love him, but I just don't feel like it.'

Suzie

'If it's not going to happen it's pointless letting him pump away. Instead I move into the 69 position so I can use my mouth and tongue to tease and stroke him. This makes him want to please me – and when he does it right, I stroke him some more. I've found when a man realises he can get mental and physical excitement from making you orgasm, you've got it made.'

Sasha

'I've never faked an orgasm. I'm twenty-one and I've only had one sexual partner, but I feel very comfortable with him. I'm a shy person normally, but when I get into a sexual situation I become a lot less inhibited in voicing my opinion. If you're lying there naked with someone there isn't much worth hiding!'

Nikki

⇥ Faking it – the biggest sin, or no big deal?

From *Company* magazine, Love in the UK Survey:

Have you ever faked an orgasm?

Yes 56%   *No* 44%

If you have faked, why?

To get it over with sooner	26%
To please him	25%
You were tired	11%
You were bored	9%
To avoid talking about why you didn't have an orgasm	3%
Soreness or pain	2%

Recognise this scenario? 'If I can hold on a bit longer,' he thinks desperately, 'she'll come too. She's obviously just about to.' She's moaning and writhing beneath him, working up to what looks like an earth-shattering peak. Then her body shudders and she cries out. 'Pretty great, eh?' he says. 'Um, yes,' she murmurs.

Except it wasn't that great. Actually she was putting on the show of her life and willing him to hurry up.

In bedrooms all over the world there's some pretty convincing faking going on – in the survey above, 56 per cent of women admitted to faking an orgasm now and again.

So why are we still doing it? 'Men think women want intercourse to last forever, but most women find that prolonged love-making does little more than make them sore, tired and bored,' says sex therapist Dr Jan Hall. Getting it over with is the most common reason why women fake it – especially if he's had a few drinks: 'Some men get what's called liquor lust, and it means he can do it all night long without having an orgasm. Many women feel if they fake it, at least they can get some sleep.'

You can argue that a quicker way to get it over with is to tell him you're not enjoying it, but most women will avoid hurting their lover at all costs, even if it means we miss out. Instead we fake, because we want to please our partners and boost their egos.

Avoiding confrontation comes into it as well. As Dr Hall says, 'Most of the things that are bad for us are easy. It's easier to keep on smoking than to give up. It's easier to fake orgasm than to talk with him about what pleases you.'

What is the harm?

What if you have an orgasm 80 per cent of the time and he has one 100 per cent of the time – is there any harm in faking it occasionally? This is very much a personal decision – no one can tell you what to do in your sex life. What's more, even the experts are divided. Dr Hall thinks it's no big deal: 'Sometimes I know, no matter what, I'm not going to make it. When that happens faking it is like telling a white lie.'

Yet clinical psychologist Eric Fleming disagrees: 'Making love isn't just about having an orgasm. He is not a failure if you don't orgasm and neither are you. In fact, the more pressure you feel to have one every time, the less likely you are to have one, and the more you'll feel you have to fake. And imagine how hurt he'll be if he ever finds out – and realises for the last ten years, when he thought you enjoyed his touch, you've been faking.'

Let's talk about sex

The ideal way to behave, according to most sex therapists, is to talk about why you didn't have an orgasm. 'You could say, well, I was about to have one, but then you asked me if I was close, and I lost it,' says Eric Fleming. 'That way you stand a chance of having one next time.'

It's best if you don't have this discussion in bed. Wait until you're both relaxed, then tell him you want to talk about your sex life together. Explain you don't always orgasm during sex, but that that's okay because you don't have to, to enjoy making love with him.

Once you've taken the pressure off one another to perform every time, you can start talking about why you're not reaching that peak. Is it because you're tired? Or is it a technique thing? If he's not doing things right, you have to be much clearer – move his hand to different parts of your body. Moan when you enjoy it, grip his hand and say, 'Yes, that's great.' Give him some feedback.

Fake it till you make it

There's also the fake-it-till-you-make-it school of thought. If you can reach orgasm through masturbation, try re-enacting the signals your body makes naturally. 'You can make your breathing quicker, make moaning noises, thrust your hips and make your vagina clench,' says Dr Hall. 'It's possible to approximate an orgasm – then move into a real one. The thing about orgasm is that once you go over the top, it's involuntary.'

All the experts (and the real-life women who wrote to *Company* magazine for this book) agree on one thing: the problem isn't going to solve itself. You need to start communicating because, ultimately, he's not responsible for your orgasm – you are. Obviously he has to at least try to give you pleasure, and not just be selfish all the time – but you also have to know how to receive pleasure. The trick is to find out what you like – probably through masturbation – then tell him about it. If you don't know how to give yourself an orgasm, how the hell's he supposed to?

➥ Ten big sex spoilers (and how to fix them)

Sex in the movies and romantic fiction is smooth and seamless. In real life sex is made up as you go along, which is why, when you expect an X-rated romp, you sometimes find yourself the reluctant star of a slapstick comedy. You try an exciting new position, only to find it gives you a pain in an unusual place. Or you flip over between the sheets . . . and fall off the end of the bed.

When things like this happen it might be comforting to know that sex therapists say that out of every ten sexual encounters with the same partner, two will be fantastic, two will be awful and the other six will be a little better or worse than average.

Even things like accidental elbows in the ribs can be part of the joy of sex. Here's how to transform them, and other sex spoilers, into pure pleasure:

Strange noises. In your mind, sex sounds like violins or two fast-beating hearts lost in passion – except all too often sex sounds like grunts, gasps and squeaks. In certain positions your vagina can break wind as well. It's normal, but can be startling if you're not expecting it.

Embarrassing noises don't have to sabotage sex. Strange noises can break the ice and help you both relax. They're also a great incentive to change sexual positions – and maybe find new ones you like.

Putting on condoms. There's no way you can really enjoy sex if you're worried about pregnancy or sexually transmitted diseases (STDs). However, safer sex has introduced a whole new area in which things can go embarrassingly wrong, which is probably why, on the whole, the subject has been ignored by Hollywood. Safer sex can be noisy, as anyone familiar with the snap, crackle and pop of a condom will know. As men tend to put condoms on while extremely excited – and in poor light – perhaps it's not surprising they can get flustered and even lose their erection. Solve the problem by putting the condom on him yourself (see page 184). Most men agree this transforms the event from a chore to a delicious part of foreplay.

Bright lighting. Passion can sneak up on you at odd times, so you may be half way through a clinch and find that a 40-watt bulb suddenly feels like a searchlight. Wanting to make love in low light does not make you a prude, so kill the electricity and light some candles instead.

He's a groaner. We say things in the heat of passion that can feel pretty silly in the cold light of day, or we make noises that would make a cat laugh, but why not revel in his groaning? You must be doing something right to get all that noise out of him. Even better, why not try joining in; it's a great libido releaser and there's nothing like a little positive feedback to make him feel like a stud.

You're stressed. Try something new. Sometimes all you need is the adventure of the unknown to get things boiling; or work up to sex after a sensual massage so you can feel calm, relaxed and raring to go.

You're angry. Talk about the problem and make up. It's a myth that sex is better when you're angry. It's more passionate when you're friends because you're both willing to try harder and you communicate and laugh more together.

You're having a fat day. It happens – but if he still desires you, who are you to argue?

You think you're a lousy lover. Or at least, not as good as his previous girlfriend. Boost your confidence by giving him a blow job. All men agree there's no such thing as bad oral sex, and you can enjoy a real kick from seeing him under your control.

You think you're not going to come. Forget about it. The more you are obsessed, the less likely it is to happen. Anyway, there's no minimum orgasm quota that says you're a sexual failure if you skip one.

You think you smell. If you don't have a vaginal infection, and you wash regularly, all you will smell of is the normal, slightly musky smell of a sexually attractive woman. Most men find this a terrific turn-on.

⇥ Silly, serious or saucy. What are you thinking during sex?

It's happened to us all. You're in the middle of making love and suddenly your mind wanders. Your partner appears lost in lust yet you're thinking, 'Do I have clean tights for tomorrow?' The fact that you can have such trivial thoughts during sex – supposedly our most intimate time – can be a trifle worrying.

The truth is, these occasional distracting thoughts aren't necessarily a problem – you may just be a bit tired one night from a hard week at work, or have too much on your mind to be able to switch off totally. However, what happens if they're becoming a common occurrence? If you have distracting thoughts three or four times in a row, relationship experts say you need to think about your relationship and what could be going on below the surface.

For example, have you fallen into something of a sexual rut? Is the problem more to do with the emotional aspect of the relationship – is he guilty of subtle put-downs about you or your looks? Perhaps you're worried about the relationship generally; do you feel he doesn't love you, or isn't putting enough into the relationship?

In all these cases you may begin to feel so resentful that you're subconsciously trying to punish him by emotionally withdrawing from sex. Experts call this process 'armouring' when you withdraw during sex as a way of protecting your feelings – you're using your distance as armour. Sometimes the process is also called 'spectatoring' because you can feel almost like another person who is watching the action from afar, a spectator rather than a participant.

Either of them will make it very difficult for you to lose yourself in sex, and as for having an orgasm, forget it. So, gradually, one of the most special parts of your relationship will become nothing but a chore. You either have to resign yourself to becoming more and more irritated and emotionally lonely – or you have to act. Here's how:

- If you're constantly plagued by distracting thoughts during sex, the crunch question is: 'Do I really want to be in this relationship?' If Yes, then there is some problem getting in the way. If No, then the distraction is a symptom, not the cause, of your unhappiness.

- Try looking outside the relationship – are there any pressures? If there aren't any long-standing or serious ones, take a good look at what you feel for your partner. What is it about his or your behaviour that could be making you feel rejected? Does he meet your needs (and not just your sexual ones)?

- Have a long talk with your partner. Find a time that's quiet, when neither of you is under pressure. To minimise angry confrontations, try the therapist's technique of only using 'I' statements – so instead of saying: 'You finish foreplay too soon,' you could say: 'I enjoy our foreplay going on longer.'

- Be very clear about how you want him to act. Even the best man isn't a thought reader and unless you let him know what's on your mind, he'll never know. Then really listen to *his* point of view – maybe you haven't been meeting his needs either and resentment has been building up on his side, making him a less thoughtful lover.

Firelighters to rekindle off days

If you have those occasional distracting thoughts during sex, therapists suggest these mental and physical techniques to help put you back on track:

Focus on the positive. To get yourself off automatic pilot during sex, try to focus on his most attractive features or the qualities that attracted you to him in the first place. Think back to the last time you had really good sex (or just a great time together) and let that glow take you over.

Fantasies aren't forbidden. If you know you are not quite in the mood, let your mind wander through your juiciest sexual fantasies. See Chapter 6 for how other women use this technique.

Change sexual gear. If you take a more active role it will concentrate your mind. Try making love partially clothed or In a different place. Think about what's being done to you – the brush of his fingers on your back, the heat of his thighs against yours. Talk intimately to him or get him to talk to you. If you usually make love with your eyes closed try opening them and staring deep into his.

Know your feelings. Avoid having sex when you're angry. If you find yourself losing interest half way through, be upfront with your partner. Change gear by having a cup of tea for fifteen minutes or a bath together. It takes the pressure off.

Is it actually your attitude? If you are feeling unhappy with your body (or sexual technique) think what you can do about it. Are you just feeling unattractive temporarily? If you can't change the problem that's niggling you (your short legs, perhaps), work on your attitude towards it. You're attractive as a person, not just a collection of body parts.

Chapter 10

SAFE SEXUAL ECSTASY

➻ When sex hurts – causes and cures

➻ How your contraception affects your pleasure

➻ How to use a condom so that it doesn't spoil the excitement – or split

➻ Alcohol – does it arouse or inhibit?

'I have had sex a few times without protection but I didn't enjoy it as much. I kept wondering if this was the night I'd fall pregnant. Men can leave, but you're the one who has to live with the consequences. It's not very relaxing.'

Iona

➻   When sex hurts

Pain during sex could be your body's way of telling you something's wrong.

Persevering when your body doesn't feel right does not make for orgasmic sex. Painful sexual experiences will, if nothing else, put you off sex, and it's all too easy to get caught in a vicious circle where previous discomfort makes you anxious – so that the next time you have sex that anxiety makes sex even more painful.

Dyspareunia, as doctors call pain during sex, is usually referred to as being superficial or deep: superficial dyspareunia refers to pain felt around the outside of the genital area and vagina; deep dyspareunia refers to pain felt deep inside the pelvis. Here are the most common reasons for both types of pain:

➻   Pain on entry

This is usually due to a dry vagina, a local infection or an allergic reaction.

1. Problem – Dry vagina

This is probably one of the most common causes of pain during sex because, if you're not properly lubricated, the action of the penis in the vagina causes irritating heat and friction (much like carpet burns). It can also cause small cuts, abrasions and even bruising in the delicate tissues, which can trigger attacks of vaginitis or cystitis.

Causes

- Too much, too soon

One cause of a dry vagina may be your partner's over-eagerness to get down to it before your body is ready. When a woman becomes sexually aroused, the walls of her vagina secrete a fluid that makes it moist and ready for her partner's penis. Just inside the vagina are the two pea-sized Bartholin's glands (one on each side) which go into overdrive during sexual excitement and secrete the fluid which coats the entrance of your vagina. If you don't feel aroused, your body will not turn itself on. How long you need to get turned on can vary, depending on the time of the month and how sexy you feel.

- Stress and worry

Changing hormone levels or different points in your menstrual cycle can make your vagina a little drier than normal, for example, just after ovulation. Water-based lubricants (available from the chemist) can help at this time. Stress can also affect the levels of hormones in your body, which can have a knock-on effect and make you more dry. First-night nerves can also play a part, and it may take a few times with the same man before you are relaxed enough to give yourself over to sex and become fully aroused.

Treatment

The more time you spend on foreplay, the better it will feel in the end. Keep the occasional not-so-great night in proportion – just because you don't get turned on once doesn't mean your sex life is doomed. Perhaps you just had a lot on your mind. Take time to relax by having hot baths, massages or whatever your favourite indulgence is. Sounds corny, but it works.

• Oral contraceptives

Although doctors disagree, some women swear their oral contraceptives can cause dryness. Certainly higher levels of progestogen do tend to make the vagina a little drier.

Treatment

There are over thirty formulations of the pill, so changing brands can probably solve the problem. If you've just started taking the pill or switched brands, allow three months for your body to adjust.

2. Problem – Vaginismus

Sometimes women have such deeply unconscious fears or anxieties about penetrative sex that the muscles in the lower part of the vagina go into spasm as soon as their partner attempts intercourse. This condition is known as vaginismus. It makes penetration uncomfortable, and in the case of some women, absolutely impossible. The muscle spasm is involuntary and many women with this condition feel as horny and frustrated as their partner.

Treatment

You may find it helpful to talk to someone trained in psychosexual matters. Your GP should be able to refer you to a local qualified counsellor.

3. Problem – Vaginal irritations

These can cause so much stinging they drive you crazy – and make sex painful. There are a number of reasons for these symptoms, all of them curable.

Causes

- Vaginitis

Candida albicans, a yeast that normally lives happily in the vagina, can be triggered into over-production at times. Such a flare-up is called vaginitis and causes a hot, burning sensation and intense irritation around the vaginal entrance, as well as a thick, white discharge which looks like cottage cheese. Vaginitis makes the skin dry and if you have sex at the start of an attack you can feel really sore afterwards. Sex when the vagina is not properly lubricated can also trigger an attack of vaginitis.

Treatment

A combined course of pessaries and cream works fast (within 24 hours). All are available without prescription at your chemist. The creams should also be rubbed into your partner's penis (especially under the foreskin), otherwise you can re-infect each other. Some women find a tampon dipped in live, natural yoghurt is also effective.

- *Trichomonas vaginalis*

These are tiny parasites which live in the vagina, and like *Candida albicans*, sometimes they can get out of hand. Symptoms are severe stinging, a strong fishy smell and a green, watery discharge. During an attack you'll probably find sex too painful to even think about – which is a good thing as the tiny cuts that would result will only make things worse.

Treatment

Consult your local genito-urinary medicine (OB/GYN) clinic. For details of the nearest, look in the phone book under hospitals. Ask the switchboard. Most major hospitals have one and you don't usually need an appointment. They'll prescribe a five-to-seven-day course of antibiotic tablets.

- Cystitis

An agonising inflammation of the bladder that causes a burning pain when you go to the toilet, as the acidic urine hits inflamed and sensitive skin. Four out of five young women suffer from cystitis at one time or another. To add insult to injury, sometimes the treatment for cystitis can trigger an attack of vaginitis.

Treatment

Cystitis can be caused by an infection. It can also be caused by bruising of the bladder tissue, often through over-enthusiastic sex or sex when the vagina is not lubricated enough (two reasons it's often called honeymoon cystitis). Making love when your bladder or bowels are full can also trigger an attack, as the movement of sex can cause uncomfortable pressure on your delicate bladder tubing. As soon as you feel cystitis coming on, drink as much water as you can. However, see your doctor if symptoms haven't disappeared after a couple of days as infections can spread to your kidneys. You'll be prescribed a course of antibiotic tablets to clear the infection.

4. Problem – Allergic reactions

Spermicidal creams can cause an allergic reaction in some women, leading to itching and swelling around the vagina. Some women (and men) can also be allergic to the spermicides used in condoms. Anything perfumed around your vagina, such as bubble baths, soaps, sprays or douches can irritate the skin madly, and cause vaginitis.

Treatment

If you suspect spermicides are the problem, try a different brand of contraceptive without spermicides. For cleansing, stick to unperfumed soaps, plain warm water or specially formulated soap-free washes such as Vagisil (available without prescription from the chemist). Douching is not a good idea. Your vagina naturally secretes all the fluids it needs to keep clean, balanced and healthy. Douching can upset this balance and cause, rather than prevent, infections and dryness.

◂▸ Deep pain inside

Sometimes the deep thrusting of sex can cause pain deep inside your body. This can be caused by a physical problem or it could be a warning of an infection of your reproductive organs. Although serious, these infections can be treated, or the symptoms lessened.

1. Problem – Just the way you're made

Deep pain inside isn't always a sign of real problems. Around the time of egg release or ovulation some women's ovaries are more sensitive and it's possible for your partner to brush against them during sex, causing a stabbing pain. Other women find their cervix gets bumped during certain positions, which can be uncomfortable. It may be that you just need to avoid certain positions at that time of the month. If the pain persists or gets worse, see your GP.

2. Problem – Cysts

Sometimes ovaries develop harmless cysts. These are relatively common and often don't cause any discomfort. Most cysts are fluid-filled sacs that develop on one or both of the ovaries. They can cause pain during intercourse, a swollen stomach or an upset monthly cycle.

Treatment

Often these cysts disappear even before you know you've had them. However, sometimes they grow to such an extent that they put pressure on the surrounding organs. In which case they need to be treated with surgery or hormone therapy.

3. Problem – Pelvic inflammatory disease (PID)

If left untreated, this can 'glue' your delicate reproductive organs together and make you sterile. It's not a rare disease either – about 100,000 cases are diagnosed in the UK every year. PID is an umbrella term for infections that have penetrated deep into the reproductive system. It can hit the ovaries (ovaritis), Fallopian tubes (salpingitis) and the uterus or womb. There are many causes, but in a large number of cases it's caused by sexually transmitted infections that have not been treated.

Although you have no discharges and, on the surface, everything seems normal, the infected area inside becomes inflamed and scar tissue can develop, causing a painful throbbing sensation during sex.

Treatment

PID is treatable, but the earlier it is caught the better. Early diagnosis means it can be treated with an appropriate course of antibiotics, bed rest and no sex. In extreme cases surgery may be necessary. Without sounding alarmist, it's worth visiting an OB/GYN clinic every time you change sexual partners because many sexually transmitted diseases can be completely symptom free. A man can be infected and yet look and feel so healthy he has absolutely no idea he has the disease – or that he is passing it on to you.

4. Problem – Endometriosis

Every month the cells that make up the lining of the womb (the endometrium) build up and then are released as the bloodflow of your period, if no fertilised egg arrives. Endometriosis arises when the cells of this tissue manage to travel outside the womb (or uterus) and begin growing elsewhere in the body. The growths are normally found in the pelvic area, on the ovaries and between the uterus and bowel, but they have been found as far away as the lining of the nose. Sometimes they lead to a build-up of scar tissue which means nearby organs can become 'glued' together. At this stage you can experience painful sex just before or after menstruation. Lower back pain is also common and many women find the only comfortable position is lying on their backs, with their knees drawn up.

Treatment

It depends on how many endometrial patches there are. The patches can be removed through various surgical techniques, or drugs can be used to shrink the cysts and minimise the pain. No one knows what causes endometriosis, and it has a tendency to reoccur, but drugs and nasal sprays are available which will reduce symptoms.

5. Problem – Ectopic pregnancy

In rare cases, an ectopic pregnancy, when the egg is lodged and growing in the Fallopian tube instead of in the stretchy womb or uterus, can cause dull pain during sex. It is not a common symptom – usually women experience mild bleeding, abdominal tenderness or missed or abnormal periods. Many women also experience normal signs of pregnancy such as swollen breasts and nausea.

Treatment

This is an emergency. If left untreated the Fallopian tube will rupture and cause a massive blood loss, even fatality. Surgery is required to remove the embryo.

6. Problem – Retroverted uterus

The uterus is usually bent slightly forwards and rests on the bladder. In about 12 per cent of women the uterus tilts slightly backwards (a retroverted uterus). Normally this isn't a problem and the woman is as fertile as anyone else. However, now and again, it can cause pain during sex.

Treatment

Try different sexual positions. If it continues to interfere, a small operation is available to correct the condition.

➡ How contraception affects your pleasure

Your choice of contraception plays a major role in your sex life – worrying about getting pregnant or catching a sexually transmitted disease are common orgasm slayers. To maximise your pleasure, make sure your contraception suits not just your lifestyle, but your sex style too. Here's what to bear in mind . . .

The contraceptive pill

Still the most popular choice of contraception for women under thirty, the pill is a great freedom-giver in long-term relationships. If you remember to take it every day the risk of pregnancy is virtually nil.

The combined pill contains oestrogen and progestogen. Together they prevent ovulation (egg release) and thicken the mucus at the top of the cervix, making it harder for sperm to get through. The mini-pill, also called the progestogen-only pill, only thickens mucus. It *must* be taken at the same time every day or it loses effectiveness. Side effects can include tender breasts, migraines and depression.

Sex style

Great for spontaneous sex, but not the best choice if you're having casual relationships as the pill offers no protection against HIV and other sexually transmitted diseases.

Orgasm potential

**** High if you're in a stable, loving relationship and not suffering from any side effects, but
* Low if you experience side effects such as tender breasts or weight gain.

Rhythm method

This works by avoiding sex on the days you're ovulating and could get pregnant. May reduce your orgasm potential. High oestrogen levels at ovulation make this the sexiest time of the month, yet you can't have sex.

Sex style

Great, if you're in a stable relationship and you both have strong will power.

Orgasm potential

** Okay, because it's a natural method, but lose a point for having to avoid sex on the four sexiest days. Worries about getting pregnant or catching STDs can make this a one-star choice.

The Intra-uterine Device (IUD) or System (IUS)

Inserted into the uterus, this works by preventing fertilised eggs from implanting. It stays in place for up to three years. Traditional IUDs can cause heavy, painful periods, but the latest hormone-releasing intra-uterine system called Mirena may eliminate cramping and result in lighter periods by releasing small amounts of the hormone progestogen.

Sex style

Same as for takers of the contraceptive pill.

Orgasm potential

**** High if there are no problems, but
* Low if you suffer cramping or heavy periods.

Diaphragm/Cap

Both are made of rubber and cover the cervix. They're
more effective when used with spermicides, which can
reduce the risk of catching STDs. However, spermicides
can also lead to allergic reactions (see page 174) leading to itching and soreness around the vagina. Although
a diaphragm can be inserted up to eight hours ahead
of sex, some women feel it can destroy the spontaneity of
sex. Others find they become prone to cystitis.

Sex style

Useful if you enjoy sex during your period as the rubber dome can hold back blood for up to six hours.

Orgasm potential

**** High if you don't experience any problems, but
* Low if you're prone to infections.

Condoms

The ultimate barrier method when used correctly
and with a spermicide: BSI kitemarked condoms have
a 98 per cent pregnancy prevention success rate – plus
you get protection from HIV and other STDs. Anti-
orgasm minuses may include an allergic reaction to

the spermicide or to latex, which can cause itching. The female condom (Femidom), which is made of polyurethane, can help in this case. A male poly-urethane condom is also available, called Avanti. Extra lubrication may also help, but choose *water-based only* as oil-based ones (like Vaseline) rot the rubber within seconds – as do some ointments, for example vaginitis creams.

Sex style

The best contraception for casual relationships

Orgasm potential

**** High but drops to
** Fairly low if you're easily embarrassed – or it splits (see page 184 for hints on how to prevent this).

Contraceptive implants

Often known by the brand name Norplant, this method uses five matchstick-sized rods which are inserted under the skin of your upper arm by a trained GP. They last for five years, releasing a low dose of a progestogen hormone. Anti-orgasm problems include headaches and loss of libido. If you normally have a high sex drive and you miss it, you may prefer to have the rods removed – your body will return to its normal cycle within a month.

Sex style

Same as the contraceptive pill, plus you don't have to think about contraception for five years.

Orgasm potential

**** High if you have a regular partner and experience no side effects, but this can drop to
* Low if the hormones cause loss of libido.

Withdrawal/Fingers crossed

Avoiding pregnancy this way (your partner pulls out just before he climaxes) is not recommended as semen can leak out before he comes, and if you're worried about pregnancy or STDs you can be too tense to enjoy yourself.

Sex style

Okay, if you're not too bothered about getting pregnant, and have total trust in your partner.

Orgasm potential

** Fair if your orgasm is reached before your partner climaxes. Otherwise you can both be so concerned to make sure he withdraws on time that all pleasure is abandoned.

➥ How to use a condom

Using a condom need not be an embarassing turn off, nor should there be any danger of it splitting if you use the correct technique. (Estate agents have a saying about what sells a house: Location, Location, Location. When it comes to keeping a condom intact the saying should be Lubrication, Lubrication, Lubrication.)

Follow these instructions and all should be well:

* Use a new condom every time you make love.

* Open the foil pack carefully to avoid tearing.

* Wait until his penis is hard enough – trying to put a condom on a slightly soft penis is like trying to get toothpaste back in the tube.

* Take the condom out of the foil and make sure it is the right way round. (You'll know if it's not. You won't be able to roll it down.)

* Put the condom over the top of his penis and gently roll the condom down. Sometimes getting it over the head is difficult so, firmly but gently, hold the head while you roll the condom over the top.

* Make sure the condom extends to the base of the penis. This is important. If it's not completely pulled down it may ruck up during intercourse and come off inside you.

* Be generous with lubrication. Spit is fine, or use a *water-based* lubricant such as K-Y Jelly (available without prescription at the chemist). Studies show the major cause of splitting is not enough lubrication, so slap it on. You can also add more half way through if you start to feel a bit dry.

- *Do not use oil-based lubricants* (such as petroleum jelly or baby oil) as they rot the condom, sometimes within seven seconds.

- Shortly after ejaculation – before his penis becomes too soft – grasp the penis and the condom near the base. Hold firmly while he pulls out of you so that the condom stays on the penis.

- Wrap the used condom in a tissue and put it in the bin. (They just won't flush down the toilet!)

➨ Alcohol and arousal

Some women find they're sexually wilder after a drink or two – yet others find their responses are dulled and they can't reach orgasm. So, why does alcohol affect women's responses so differently?

Even the experts aren't sure. In one survey 60 per cent of women said alcohol made them less inhibited, and 45 per cent found it made sex more pleasurable. However, most of these changes could be in our imaginations. When female volunteers watched an erotic film, most of them said they didn't feel very turned on, and felt much 'hotter' after two or three drinks. However, vaginal arousal clues (such as increased bloodflow and secretions) proved that their sexual responsiveness was actually lowered after the drinks, and heightened after the film.

This may explain why women who drink more than the equivalent of a large vodka and tonic take longer to reach orgasm. Our minds may be willing, but our bodies aren't.

On the other hand, the same research discovered that although orgasm can take longer to reach, we enjoy it more when it happens. This might be because a drink makes us feel less self-conscious.

Other experts believe the answer lies in our hormones. Small amounts of alcohol can cause a dramatic but temporary surge of the male sex hormone testosterone, which can increase sexual desire. The effect is strongest in women on the contraceptive pill, who have low testosterone levels, or women who are not on the pill but who are ovulating.

Above all, if you believe you're sexy, you'll feel sexy. By enjoying a glass of wine we think we have a licence to be more wild and sexually excited – and so we are. It has very little to do with the alcohol and everything to do with our attitude.

Chapter 11

NOW IT'S OVER TO YOU . . .

I'm going to leave the final words to two of the *Company* magazine readers who so generously and frankly responded to the request for details of their sex lives for this book.

They seem to have found the recipe for sexual fulfilment – I hope that this book will help you to the same happy and enjoyable climax.

'First I have "butterfly" sensations in my pelvis and vagina. My body is rigid and my breathing is affected – it's almost as if I have to hold my breath. I must be completely still to concentrate on the sensations building up. My clitoris is hard, my vagina tightens and so do the muscles around my cervix. My body is very tense and I know I am going to have an orgasm as soon as I feel a deep, almost unbearable internal "tickling" sensation. The orgasm is quite violent but a very pleasurable release (the nearest I can describe it is like water suddenly breaking through a dam wall). I then have about six or seven deep vaginal muscular contractions in which my vagina tightens. The outside of my vagina and clitoris swell and pulsate with each contraction. At the moment of climax my breathing stops and I feel my body will explode from the pressure.

Afterwards my heartbeat is very evident and there is a reddish rash around my neck and chest.'

Joanna

'My orgasm feels physical and mental together. Mentally I feel I'm in heaven; physically, it's the most amazing feeling on earth. Afterwards I feel warm, very happy, sensual and complete.'

Suzie